1 MONTH OF
FREE
READING

at

www.ForgottenBooks.com

By purchasing this book you are eligible for one month membership to ForgottenBooks.com, giving you unlimited access to our entire collection of over 1,000,000 titles via our web site and mobile apps.

To claim your free month visit:

www.forgottenbooks.com/free526571

ISBN 978-0-483-68675-5
PIBN 10526571

A

PLEA

FOR

INFANT BAPTISM,

IN SEVEN PARTS.

I. *The Standing Authority of the Old Testament.*
II. *The Grace of the Abrahamic Covenant.*
III. *The permanent sanction of the Moral Law.*
IV. *The subjects and mode of Christian Baptism.*
V. *An Address to Anabaptists.*
VI. *An Address to Pædobaptists.*
VII. *An Address to the Undetermined.*

——— ✳✳✳ ———

By JAMES MILLIGAN,

Pastor of the Reformed Presbyterian Societies in Ryegate, Topsham, Barnet and Craftsbury.

——— ✳✳✳ ———

But Jesus said, suffer little children, and forbid them not, to come unto me, for of such is the kingdom of heaven.—JOHN xix. 14.

——— ✳ ———

DANVILLE:

PRINTED BY EBENEZER EATON.

• • • • • • • •

1818.

SALUTATION.

To the candid Christian Reader—
Grace be with you, mercy and peace from
God the Father, and from the Lord
Jesus Christ, the Son of the Fa-
ther in truth and love.

INTRODUCTION

IN sending this work abroad, the author is aware that it is a contested subject. He is also sensible that in this age, controversy is, with many, rather unfashionable. It is particularly to be regretted that defence of ancient truth, principle and order seems to be especially decreed.

The religious world has been, for a long time in a revolutionary state, and although factions multiply, animosities do, in some measure seem to subside. This must certainly be pleasing to all the lovers of peace. It is, however, very natural for society to oscillate between extremes.

The social orb has been for a considerable time in the cold regions of the north. Scepticism and indifference about principle have succeeded to blind zeal and bloody persecution.

Those who used, while power was in their hands, to be most active in such work are now the most noisy advocates of forbearance, moderation and charity. This they need not do, to dull the edge of the sword, or quench the violence of the flame, which they used to wield and kindle, but they wish to ward off, thereby, the spiritual weapons which the advocates of truth and scriptural order use against their crazy systems.

This is improper, unfair and cowardly. The best time to adjust differences among parties is a time of peace. We do not need, however, to charge the Baptist brethren with these extremes. They have never persecuted ; they have never been remiss. They have generally manifested a zeal worthy of a good cause in promoting the interest of their society and in propagating the peculiar tenets of their sect. For this they deserve credit. Let every one be fully persuaded in his own mind ; and whatever any man's hand finds to do, let him do it with all his might. If they are wrong, I do not justify them for that ; but if they are right, they ought to be zealous against all others who must on that supposition be radically and fundamentally wrong.

If they are mistaken, and yet think themselves exclusively correct, they are consistent in using all their zeal and strength in vindicating the supposed truth and order which they defend. At all events it must be considered a matter of sufficient magnitude to engage the attention of all the friends of truth, propriety and peace.

It is the importance of the subject, christian and candid reader, that justifies my appearance at your bar. The cause which I plead is the cause of the poor defenceless children of credible believers. They come into the world naked as well as others, and need as well as others, regeneration. Natural descent from christian parents does not communicate to them sanctifying grace. Still if the great Redeemer's Rule of the Church has ordained that they shall be covered with the skirt of parental representation, and be dandled on the knees of the church in infancy, you will not count me a disturber of your repose while I plead their cause.

In pleading this too, if it appears that the covenant charter really makes such provision for the infants of such as are members of the visible church that they are to be baptised : then I shall be pleading the cause not only of babes, but also of God. If he really has ordained that children be members of the visible church by the represen. tation of their parents ; it is certainly indignant treatment of Him to say that they shall not.

The advocates upon the other side of the controversy must give me credit for honesty of intention—for vindicating ancient claims—and the cause of mercy. They cannot say that I have undertaken this suit by the misrepresentation of high fees of my infant clients. No, poor things, they are mute, and if concerned, it is about something else than their great birth-right. To this it is true they have no right upon the footing of the covenant of works. By this, on the contrary, misery and death have devolved upon all the apostate family. Hence we see those who have not sinned after the similitude of Adam's transgression, i. e. who have not actually sinned are liable to death. We do, however humbly presume that our great Saviour, has in his clemency and mercy revealed a covenant, whereby he may yet have a holy nation; a godly seed. The baptism of infants is not regeneration : nor does it avail to the purifying of the flesh. Yet we hope, by divine

A 2

aid, to prove that it may be to well informed parents the answer of a good conscience towards God. It is particularly to be desired that this controversy should be fairly settled; in order that one great obstacle may be removed which stands in the way of a general union among professors. There are several causes of present existing divisions, which it is easy to see, may vanish without any particular determination, which of the parties is now correct. Some view in the general diffusion of evangelical light may be so clear, absorbing and effulgent, that the parties may readily and amicably drop the dispute about those which were previously peculiar. Like mariners and wanderers, who in the dark night dispute about stars glimmering through the clouds; or lights occasionally gleaming through the bazy way, when the rolling sun arises in his purple majesty in the east, the controversy ends.

But this cannot be the case in this dispute. Either the infants of professors must be considered as having, or not having, a right to membership in the Church, or there can be no Millenial union. As the members of the church of Christ, are all not only made of, but also redeemed by one blood, inhabited by one Spirit, and travelling to one heavenly country, it would certainly be agreeble to all of that community that they should see eye to eye in the great doctrines and duties of religion, and speak with the voice together in a harmonious, holy and united profession.

There is really but *one* Lord, *one* faith and *one*

baptism. Why then are professors not visibly and formally united? Why do the subjects of one Lord quarrel? Why do the heirs of like precious faith disagree about forms? Bodily exercise profitteth little : Godliness is profitable unto all things, having the promise of the life that now is and of that which is to come. Still it must be admitted that the best way to obtain unity in principle and uniformity in practice is to adhere closely and strictly to divine institution. ' To the law and to the testimony. If they speak not according to the word it is because there is no light in them.' Isa. viii. 20. Can two walk together except they be agreed. Amos iii. 3. What Christ has considered of sufficient importance to reveal, we should not rashly call indifferent to believe and profess—what he has commanded, we ought unquestionably to observe and do. If Episcopalians, Congregationalists and Presbyterians have no authority for baptising infants, they ought candidly to confess their error and desist from their unauthorised practice. Better to reform than be always wrong, and the sooner reformation is effected the more honorable and the more advantageous. If they have authority, it is certainly due to the Baptist brethren that these other denominations should exhibit their authority, and render a reason for their hope. i. e. If children are included in the new covenant charter, of which baptism is the visible initiatory seal, let the evidence thereof be produced, and let all concerned give unprejudiced attention.

That this subject may have a fair hearing is the design of the following plea ; and that it may tend, by the blessing of God, to edify Christians and unite the Churches is the sincere desire and fervent prayer of

THE AUTHOR.

A
PLEA

FOR

INFANT BAPTISM, &c.

PART I.

IT is proper in all controversies, that the disputants should have certain first principles upon which they agree, and to which they may refer the points in debate. Unhappily, however, in this dispute, as in many others of modern date, first principles themselves have been denied. Protestants of all denominations used to admit that the great judge in all theological trials was the Spirit of God speaking in the scriptures of the Old and New Testaments—that the covenant of grace was one and the same in all ages, although variously dispensed.

We should be glad if the sceptical extravagance of modern times would allow us still to assume these truths as axioms. But the case is otherwise. We submit. Let the New Testament then decide. Let it be understood, however, that if we prove from the New Testament the divinity and standing authority of the Old, we shall then have it in our power to draw from that source arguments in proof of our plea. Mathematicians frequently refer to their demonstrations; as well as to their primary axioms and postulates. It will not then be denied that the Old Testament scriptures were once given by divine inspiration and under divine sanction.

If the Lord did not speak to Moses and to all the Prophets, they must be reckoned horrid imposters, because they most explicitly gave out that he did. There is but one alternative. If the Lord then did not speak to Moses and the prophets, and by them to the Fathers, then Moses must be accounted a greater imposter than the prophet of Mecca; and if the Lord did speak to them, then they who say he did not must be worse than Mahomet himself, for he admitted that Moses was a prophet.

Again—if the Old Testament writings were given under the sanction of divine authority as a rule of faith and manners, they must be allowed that place until equal or paramount authority abolish their claim. Did the Son of God, when in our nature, raised up from among the brethren the great prophet of the Church, do this? Have the Apostles, endowed with the Holy Spirit of Jesus Christ, done it?

Let us examine these points. Here we are aware that we are rather deviating from established rules of controversy, and taking the place of our opponents. If we find the law, they should find the exceptions, or the repeal. The burden of proof rests upon the affirmant. If they say these writings are obsolete, they ought to prove it. However, as we are enquiring for truth, we are willing not to stand upon points. We would rather labor a little out of order to prove two negatives than be found striving to prove one falsehood.

The first text then we use to prove that the old Testament scriptures are yet of standing authority is John v. 39 —"Search the scriptures, for in them ye think ye have eternal life, and they are they which testify of me." Here it is evident and indisputable that the scriptures of which he here speaks are the scriptures of the Old Testament. This was in the very commencement of his ministry, when there were no other scriptures in existence. Now we would ask the candid opponent if it be likely, on the supposition of the truth of his plea, that the divine teacher would speak in this manner of scriptures, the authority and utility of which he was come to abolish. It is true he does not say that in them they had eternal life, but in them ye think ye have. If they were wrong, however, in thinking so, it certainly would have been kind to have corrected their error, and said—Never trouble yourselves with these old writings : I am come to repeal them. You shall soon have scriptures, which without these superanuated ones will be sufficient. How contrary to this is the text and the context. v. 45— Do not think that I will accuse you to the Father, there is one that accuseth you, even Moses, in whom ye trust ; for had ye believed Moses, ye would have believed me, for he wrote of me ; but

if ye believe not his writings, how can ye believe
my words ? In like manner in his sermon on the
Mount, he says—Matth. v. 17, Think not that I
am come to destroy the law and the prophets ;
I am not come to destroy, but to fulfill : For verily I say unto you, till heaven and earth shall pass
one jot or one tittle shall in no wise pass from the
law, till all be fulfilled. Whosoever therefore
shall break one of the least of these commandments and shall teach men so, shall be called the
least in the kingdom of heaven ; but whosoever
shall do and teach them shall be called great in the
kingdom of heaven. The same solemn ratification of the old testament writings is pronounced
by the lips of our risen Redeemer. See the colloquy between him and the two disciples travelling to Emmaus, Luke xxiv. 25—Then he said
unto them, O fools, and slow of heart to believe
all that the prophets have spoken. v. 26. Ought
not Christ to have suffered these things, and to
enter into his glory ? And beginning at Moses,
and all the prophets, he expounded unto them in
all the scriptures the things concerning himself.

This was perfectly in unison with the instruction he had delivered to them before his suffering.
Now in the period between his resurrection and
ascension, he teaches them very particularly how
they are to transact the business of his kingdom
and still he shews the greatest respect for the old
testament writings. After he had been made
known to them by breaking bread at Emmaus,
and again saluted them in their evening meeting

at Jerusalem, he says, v. 44. These are the words which I spake unto you, while I was yet with you, that all things must be fulfilled which were written in the law of Moses, and in the prophets, and in the Psalms, concerning me. All these things were plainly enough revealed in the scripture; the only desideratum was, to have the mind illuminated. This the divine teacher supplied; "Then opened he their understanding, that they might understand the scriptures, and said unto them; Thus it is written, and thus it behoved Christ to suffer, and to rise from the dead the third day." You see from this plainly that it must have been another than the divine teacher that has preached down the Old Testament, and it must be in another association than in the kingdom of heaven, or christian Church that this abolition has taken place.

Again. What do the Apostles say upon this subject? Do they say that, being appointed to establish the church upon the New Testament plan, they deny the authority of the Old Testament scriptures? No; on the contrary, they quote them and submit what they say to be tried by them. They recommend the individuals and Churches which searched these venerable documents and put their doctrines to the test of Old Testament authority. Turn your attention to a few of the many instances which might be adduced in proof of this fact. Acts xvii. 11—These were more noble than those in Thessalonica, in that they received the word with all readiness of mind, and searched the scriptures daily, whether

B

these things were so. Here again, we have the
old testament writings called by their appropriate
epithet, the scriptures, and the Berean believers
honoured for their diligent attention to the instruction contained in them. Yea, they are more
noble than the believers in Thessalonica, because
they compared the verbal instruction of the Apostles, whose word they received, with the written
authoritative documents of the Old Testament.
It must not be overlooked, that the teacher here
was the Apostle of the Gentiles, and although he
preached in the synagogue both here and at Thessalonica, yet he had Gentile auditors, for ladies of
honorable rank, who were Greeks, and of men not
a few, believed. All this, however, was perfectly
natural and consistent, for he reasoned out of the
scriptures, aud therefore allowed and invited all
his auditors, of course, to have their bibles, and
search daily from these authentic and divine
writings of the Old Testament, whether or not
his reasoning was fair. He wished to urge upon
them no article of faith, nor rule of practice which
did not accord with God's consistent word.

The next passage to which we solicit the candid
reader's attention is in 1 Cor. ix. In that chapter,
and indeed in a great part of the epistles addressed to the Corinthians there is some obscurity a-
bout the particular bearing of the Apostle's reasoning, because we have not the other side of the
correspondence ; still, there is no obscurity as to
his opinion touching the point in hand. He is in
the beginning of this chapter pleading the right

which he and Barrabas had to remuneration or support in their ministerial labors, and after having reasoned from common principles of justice, he appeals to still higher authority. "Say I these things as a man, or sayeth not the law the same also. 9. For it is written, thou shalt not muzzle the mouth of the ox that treadeth out the corn : Doth God take care for oxen ? or saith he it altogether for our sakes ? For our sakes no doubt this is written." Here you see the apostle establishes Old Testament authority and utility, not only to us as well as Old Testament saints, but also that it is particularly useful to us.

I providentially glance upon another passage, Eph. ii. 20. And are built upon the foundation of the Apostles and *Prophets*, Jesus Christ himself being the chief corner stone. In all things He must have the pre-eminence. If the writer then had any design in the arrangement, the prophets are nearest him who was before Abraham. However, here the Church is considered under the notion of a temple or holy building, to be a habitation of God by the Spirit. Upon what is this building founded ? Upon the Apostles ; what does this mean ? Is it not that they believed their words, and obeyed their inspired precepts and example? Well, but the Church is built upon the prophets also ; and so it is evident that, whatever be the faith of modern Churches respecting the Old Testament, primitive Christians believed it, and endeavored to obey it. The Apostles put the prophets upon a par with themselves. That they were quickened by the Spirit, and were new creatures by the grace of Christ, did not divert their attention from the law of Christ. They knew that the testimony of Jesus was the spirit of prophecy, and therefore to that spirit and testimony they would give diligent heed. By this means they who had been waiting to see the accomplishment of their prophecies, were gratified, and the astonished beholders of all these recent events, were no less gratified and confirmed in beholding that all these things had been foretold.

We have seen transiently what was the faith of the apostles and the churches immediately planted by their hands upon this important point. Let us now see what the faith of those was; unto whom they committed the trust of building on the edifice which they founded. Timothy was by descent partly Jewish, partly Grecian, i. e. a Greek was his father, and a Jew was his mother. He was ordained by the laying on of the hands of the presbytery, a minister of Christ. He was left by the apostle Paul at Ephesus, that he might charge some that they should teach no other doctrine. He receives very particular charge to be choice of the characters, whom he might be instrumental of inducting into the ministerial office. " The same commit thou to faithful men, who shall be able to teach others also." What then was his faith upon this subject? The apostle tells us that it was the same which dwelt first in his grandmother Lois and mother Eunice. ii. Tim. 1; 5. His fe-

male predecessors were careful to instruct him in
the doctrines of salvation early, and their labour
was blessed. , They not only instructed a pupil for
heaven, but they educated an evangelist who was
to conduct others thither. What was the supreme standard of their faith and system of religious instruction ? Why, truly the scriptures.
ii. Tim. iii. 15. And that from a child thou
hast known the holy scriptures, which are able to
make thee wise unto salvation. The Apostle in
that chapter seems to have had a very vivid picture of present times before him. This know,
says he, that in the last days, perilous times shall
come; men shall be lovers of their own selves,
covetous, boasters, proud, blasphemers. 2, 13.
But evil men and seducers shall wax worse and
worse, deceiving and being deceived. 14. But
continue thou in the things which thou hast learned, and hast been assured of, knowing of whom
thou hast learned them. Seducers and heretics
are generally first deceived themselves. This
does not excuse them. It is always a very suspicious character, that would have men renounce
the religious principles, in which they have been
taught. It ought not to be done without serious
and candid examination. It is admitted that a
doctrine is not true, because my forefathers believed it and taught it to me; but it is also true,
that it is not therefore false, and it argues a very
base and ungrateful mind, to renounce, without
careful investigation, the principles, which pious
and witnessing ancestors believed and perhaps

sealed with their blood. . Those who are themselves unsteadfast and wavering, and who wish to
influence spirits akin to themselves, may do so ;
but those who desire to say, let us go on to per-
fection in finishing a testimony, will not cast away
the labors and attainments of ancient times, until
they have better to put in their room ; or until
they condense the past, with well digested additions, amendments and improvements. But so it
is—one man is famous for saying, hold fast the
form of sound words, and another for crying
down creeds and confessions ;—one for lifting up
his axe against the thick trees to prepare materi-
als for the temple of truth ; another for going a-
gainst the same magnificent fabric, with axes and
hammers to destroy the carved work.

. We must not, however, make them worse than
they are. It is not that their followers should
have no professional lodging or creed at all ; but
it is that they may not have one so high, so luminous, as ancient mansions. Like the very wise
and sympathetic Tartar, living in his cell, his door
and chimney all the same, when he heats of two
story houses, he pities the folk that are so scarce
of ground that they must build houses in the air.
In general you will find those reformers, that want
to destroy all confessions and forms of sound
words, making such as the following their confession : Art. 1.—There should be no confession
of faith but the scriptures. 2.—Christ died for
all men, to open a way for the salvation of all who
will repent and believe. 3—If any should not

agree with the foregoing confession he may unite
with us, if he comes possessed of a christian spirit, i. e. be friendly towards us in our loose way.
Such are always very much opposed to rational
deductions, if they militate against their favorite
opinions; but have no objections to infer, perhaps
sometimes wreck inference, and wrest scripture,
forge terms and manufacture logic in order to
carry a point. Upon such novices, however, the
evangelist must not speedily lay his hand. They
are like Jannes and Jambres, who withstood Moses. So do they also resist the truth, men of
corrupt minds, reprobate concerning the faith.—
II. Tim. iii. 8.

In like manner, Paul exhorts Titus, when employed in furnishing the churches with proper
teachers. Thus they are described as—" Holding fast the faithful word as he hath been taught,
that he may be able by sound doctrine, both to
exhort and to convince the gainsayers."—Titus
1, 9. Now what was that faithful word in which
they had been taught? I do not say that it has
no reference to the New Testament, but if it excludes the Old, it would be well to prove, as well
as to say it. It must be remarked too, that there
are elders who are spoken of. Nor are we to
suppose that Paul in all this was judaizing from
the prejudice of his own education. No; he
charges them against giving heed to Jewish fables and commandments of men, that *turn* from
the truth. v. 14. These two epistles may be
considered as lessons apostolical and divine, ad-

dressed to the teachers of the Church in every age,
and if there be any thing in them which so much as
implies disrespect to the authority of the Old Testament scriptures, I really cannot see it. I do not
think Timothy or Titus did, and I question very
much if Paul intended it. But the subject is
rather solemn, and we are all so fallible in our
judgments, that there should be great allowance,
if men would keep in any bounds ; but when men
will cry and cut themselves with knives, saying,
Baal save us, what can we do but say ' cry aloud.'

What are we to say on the epistle to the Hebrews ?

This is by all considered the great bond which
visibly connects the Old and New Testament
writings. Mark its beginning—God, who at sun-
dry times and in divers manners, spake unto the
prophets, hath in these latter days spoken to us by
his own Son. Heb. i: 1, 2. Although the scriptures were given at different times, and in divers
manners, still it was God that spoke, perfectly cor-
roborating what we ought to have noticed before
in the 16th verse of Timothy iii. All scripture is
given by inspiration of God, and *is* profitable for
doctrine, for reproof, for correction and instruction in righteousness, that the man of God may
be perfect, thoroughly furnished unto all good
works. In the most of Paul's epistles he asserts
his Apostolic authority; but in this he is reasoning with those who believe the Old Testament
scriptures, and therefore he immediately joins
issue with those in proving the divinity of Jesus.

His eminence as a teacher above Moses, as a priest above Aaron, as a king above David. He is Lord of the house, and so above all the builders and above the house itself. Note, we say, he proves all these from the *Old Testament scriptures*, and could the Apostle reason from a book whose authority he, or any partaking of the same spirit, with which he was endowed, would deny? Yea, he proves, particularly by a citation from the xxxi. of Jer. that God would ratify a new covenant with them. Not new as to its substance, as we design afterwards to shew, but in the mode of its application, being more eminently inward. He would write his law on their heart. He would be their God and they should be his people indeed and in truth! For unto us was the gospel preached, as well as unto them. Heb. iv. 2. If it be thought necessary we can shew that James and Peter speak in the same style about the old Testament scriptures, that we have seen Jesus, Luke, and Paul do: Jas. ii. 23. And the scripture was fulfilled, which saith—"Abraham believed God, and it was imputed to him for righteousness, and he was called the friend of God."

What scripture is this which Jas. quotes with such respect? The first assertion is found in the book of the Old Testament. Gen. v. 6. The second is found in a book, which, if any of the old Testament writings should be considered obsolete, it should, viz. 2 Chron. xx. 7. Yet from both of these ancient books the apostle James quotes and calls them scripture, and that to prove a doctrine at

once evangelical and practical. Jas. iv. 5. In
citing apostolic authority for the Old Testament
scriptures, we must not altogether neglect Peter.
Hear then what he says, referring to Isa. xxviii.
16. and Psal. cxviii. 22.—Wherefore also it is
contained in the *scripture ;* Behold I lay in Zion
a chief corner stone, elect precious, and he that
believeth on him shall not be confounded. Unto
you then which believe he is precious : but unto
them which be disobedient, the stone which the
builders disallowed, the same is made the head of
the corner, and a stone of stumbling and a rock of
offence, even to them which stumble at the *word,*
being disobedient. 1 Pet. ii. 6, 7, 8. In the iii.
chap. 12 v. he quotes also from Psalm xxxiv. 15.
For the eyes of the Lord are over the righteous,
and his ears are open to their prayers ; but the
face of the Lord is against them that do evil.' He
expressly declares that the same spirit by which
these elect strangers were quickened, preached by
Noah to the disobedient Antedeluvians, whose
spirits were now in prison. v. 18, 19, 20. He
calls the Old Testament administration and scriptures the gospel. chap. iv. 6—"For, for this cause
was the *gospel* preached unto them also that are
dead, that they might be judged according to men
in the flesh, but live according to God in the spirit." This passage contains a mass of information
and proof of our plea. He is encouraging the
believers of his own time to patience and christian
fortitude under the sore persecutions and fiery
trials of their time. 1. From the example of

Christ. 2. From the example of ancient saints, long since deceased. " That they might be judged &c. 3. From the circumstance that they had not only the external gospel, but also the internal administration thereof by the spirit. Again, in the 2d epistle 1st chapter 16 v. he refers to the glorious display of Christ's divinity, which was made on the mount of transfiguration, assuring them that the gospel was not a human device. " For we have not followed cunningly devised fables, when we made known unto you the power and coming of our Lord Jesus Christ; but were eye-witnesses of his majesty. 17. For he received from God the Father, honor and glory, when there came such a voice from the excellent glory, This is my beloved Son, in whom I am well pleased. And this voice which came from heaven, we heard, when we were with him on the holy mount.' This was certainly very high authority—an Apostle declaring that he was an eye and an ear witness of the majesty and glory of the Saviour. There is authority yet higher, or evidence yet more sure, viz. the writings of the Old Testament prophets. We must give attention to it. It is a light to direct us until we pass through the dark defiles of this nocturnal-state. We are not wresting it from its proper use by so doing, for it never was designed only for temporary and partial application, and a reason and proof is assigned, that it was divinely inspired. 19. We have a more sure word of prophecy, whereunto ye do well that ye take heed as unto a light that shineth in a dark place, until the day dawn, and the day-star arise in your hearts; knowing this first, that no prophecy of the scripture is of any private interpretation. For the prophecy came not in old time by the will of man; but holy men of God spake as they were moved by the Holy Ghost. He foretells the fact, however, which makes all this reasoning necessary, viz. that there would be false teachers in New Testament times, as there had been false prophets in the Old, who, though they should seem to be reformed by the knowledge of Christ, would afterwards turn from the holy commandment that was delivered unto them, for it is happened unto them according to the true proverb; The dog is turned to his vomit again, and the sow that was washed to her wallowing in the mire. Thus it must be more than obvious, that they who deny the authority of the Old Testament scriptures to serve an end, have not done denying; they must deny the New also, and then they will rank among deists at once, and neither deceive their votaries nor pester their opponents with proving those things which ought among professors to be acknowledged facts, and principles admitted. However, they do good; their conduct is a fulfilment of prophecy, and will help to confirm the faith of God's chosen. Jude, while he exhorts to contend earnestly for the faith once delivered to the saints, describes those of another character. Enoch also, the seventh from Adam, prophecied of them. Jude v. 4—14. So also John, in Revelations xxii. 19. If any man shall take away from the words of the book of this prophecy, God shall take away his part out of the book of life and out of the holy city, and from the things which are written in this book.

It must now be remembered that unless our opponents overthrow all the foregoing reasons, we will afterwards in the subsequent parts of this plea, take it for granted that Christ did not come to destroy the law and the prophets, and that although the Spirit was sent to take of the things that are Christ's and shew them to his people, to make them new creatures in him, it is not by making them to be without law, but putting the law into their inward parts, and writing it in their hearts. He will be their God in covenant to save them, and they shall be his people to love, fear and serve him forever.

From the discussion of this part, we may learn, First. In what order the scripture should be read. Second. The desperate nature of the cause, and the dangerous character of the system which rejects the Old Testament scriptures. Third. The manner of rightly understanding the scriptures.

There is, you will at once perceive, an admirable wisdom in the arrangement of the word of God. That which we see around us is accounted for. Natural and moral phenomena are explained and connected. The history of the creation of all things—the fall of man—the dispersion of the aboriginal tribes—the catastrophe which brought men again within a narrow circle, and left such

C

permanent vestiges of universal devastation, are
all matters of such general interest and enquiry
as every liberal and curious mind will want to understand ; and how are they to know satisfactorily
these things if they do not pay early attention to
the documents provided by the ancient of days,
who is the same in all the vicissitudes of man,
and of nature ?

The spirit which vilipends these sacred relicts
of antiquity, is not only irreligious, but also bar-
barous.   Akin to this was the genius which destroyed the Alexandrian library.   The Mahome-
tan did not deny the ancient excellency of the
scriptures, but they were so completely, idola-
trously and exclusively attached to the Alcoran,
that no other book, human or divine, of more ancient date, was considered useful.   The trial was
short, and the sentence to the flames.   Either this
book contains the same of the Koran, or something different : if the former, it is useless ; if the
latter, it is dangerous.

The same spirit of illiberality and barbarity
prevailed in the dark ages of reigning popery,
when enthusiastic professors washed out the ink
of many ancient volumes of interesting matter,
and wrote upon the washen parchments the lives
of their saints.

This view of the standing authority of the Old
Testament does not establish the ancient ritual,
in its literal observance, but in its spirit and evangelical import as expounded by the New Testament.   It seems indeed almost incredible how

any person can draw such an inference, seeing the inspired men who were most active and instrumental in abrogating the observation of the one, were also zealous in establishing the authority of the other. The fair conclusion to be drawn, is, that the scripture is all of divine inspiration, and is retained and preserved for the important purpose of general edification, but that every part of it is to be taken and viewed in connection with every other, and so used for the particular end designed. The typical, legal and prophetical parts of scripture were in some sense particularly useful to those who lived when they were first given. They had then no other scriptures, and no doubt God's chosen had their eyes opened to behold the wonders of his law, and so it was found perfect to convert and edify the soul. They are particularly useful to us in another point of view. We see their accomplishment in the writings of the New Testament in the history of the nations and of the Church, and so upon us the ends of the world of divine illumination have met. What then must be our portion, if in the beam of such objective light, we are found subjectively and practically in darkness. Let us then read all the scriptures humbly, thankfully, believingly and obediently. The first of these sentiments should be inspired and cherished, by a sense not only of the inadequacy of natural reason to discover saving truth, but also of the necessity when a revelation is made, of enjoying the operation of the Spirit, to open our benighted eyes to behold the

light of the knowledge of the glory of God, in the
face of Jesus Christ. How thankful should we
be that we enjoy such means. Mysteries which
were hid from the foundation of the world have
been revealed. If they are hid it is to the lost,
whose eyes the god of this world has closed. If
these are a stumbling block to the Jew, and foolish-
ness to the Greek, they are the wisdom of God to
the salvation of them that believe. Thanks then
be to God "for his unspeakable gift." The faith
with which all the scriptures should be read, respects more than the verity and authenticity of the
scriptures, viz. the divinity of their subject, who
is Jesus Christ, of whom Moses and the Prophets,
and the Psalms all spake. His character and
achievements are revealed to our faith ; himself
and salvation to our reception. By him we become sons of God, and heirs of eternal life.

Shall we not then, as redeemed with the precious blood of Christ, study to honour him, in all
relations aud stations of life, being steadfast, un-
moveable, always abounding in the work of the
Lord, knowing that our labor shall not be in vain
in the Lord.

May the spread of the bible in its letter be accompanied with a diffusion of its spirit and power, that so its principles may be accurately known,
its sanctifying influence in the heart be felt, and
its ameliorating influence on society be universal-
ly seen. To this wish and prayer, we have no
doubt every Christian will cordially subscribe his
assent, and devoutly affix his—AMEN.

PART II.

WE have only a very succinct account of the nature of the divine dispensation with adult or infant man in the Antedeluvian age and in the subdeluvian until the days of Abraham, who is called the father of the faithful.

Learned men are of different opinions with regard to those early times, in many points. Whether they had any written annals, has been among other things controverted.

One thing we know, that whatever means of evangelical instruction they enjoyed, to which we have not access, that was not considered of importance to us. The discoveries which the voice of God made to Adam, when he announced the gospel promise that the seed of the woman should bruise the head of the serpent—the institution and signification of the typical sacrifices, which represented the lamb slain from the foundation of the world would no doubt be contemplated with great interest by these patriarchial sages, and be transmitted, with peculiar care to their numerous successive progeny.

Methinks I see the pristine sage himself, at once the teacher, priest and ruler of his numerous descendants, binding in their sight the devoted victim, and with tears in his eyes explaining to them the reason and meaning of this strange ap-

C 2.

parent cruelty. Ah! says he, "behold the effects of my first sin, by which death hath been brought into the world, and all our woe : by this as well as by our actual sins, I and all my posterity are bound over to death. But lo, with a smile bursting through the cloud of grief, and showers of sorrow, he cries, "Behold the typical substitute." And sprinkling himself and his offspring with the blood of the sacrifice, they are called by the name of Jehovah, and extol in raptures of wondering joy the name of their redeeming God. The night advances. They draw near, with hearts sprinkled from an evil conscience, and bodies washed with pure water, to present their evening acknowledgements. Beneath the shade of some lofty wide spread citron, entwined with the pliant vine, they participate a refreshing meal ; reclining for repose under the sable curtain of night, and wrapt in the skins of the sacrifice, the Father still teaches them lessons of saving import. Ah! says he, By my sin you and I became naked to our shame ; but lo, the imputed righteousness of the promised seed, the second representative is for a covering from the storm, and the rain of this present dark and dismal night. In this, then, let us repose, until the eternal day shall dawn upon us in the beatific rays of which we shall be gloriously clad and everlastingly happy.

We should egregriously err, however, should we imagine there were then many preachers of such righteousness. No, the great man of men were plotting their licentious & ambitious projects

even while the ark was a building, which was 120
years : and after this period, while all the terrible'
vestiges of that catastrophe stared the subsequent
generations wide in the face. The world after
the flood is as mad as it was before. Their ambition yet towers—their hearts are towards their
idols—they follow their own sinful ways—their
counsels and their tongues are judicially divided
to prevent the execution of one sinful and silly device—they scatter to plan and execute more—
they multiply colonies and colonial deities. God,
however, will have a seed to serve him, on whom
he may mark his name, as the sheep of his pasto-
ral care. Abraham is for this purpose called
from Ur of the Chaldees. As one of his chosen
sheep he hears his voice—he follows his shepherd,
he knows not whither. It is enough that he hears
the voice of the illustrious leader, saying, " This
is the way."

It is true he has no posterity when he starts
with his kinsman and wife, yet this covenant is
made with him and his seed. It is proper that
we should now consider this covenant, its seal, its
promise. The words by which making a covenant was expressed, *chere cheteb*, signify to cut the
sacrifice, or divide the purifier. Doubtless the
idea of the word, and the phraseology are derived from the ancient and general rites performed
in making treaties or covenants; the parties passed through the bloody divided victim, invocating
such curses, divisions & death upon themselves, if
they brake the stipulations of the solemn partion.

The kind of animal which, according to the taste of the nation, was considered peculiarly excellent for food, was generally used.

Hence we find the Greeks and the Romans bisecting the swine.—The Jews cutting the calf in twain. Whence the practice originated the reflecting mind will not be at a loss to tell. No doubt the typical beasts which the great highpriest of our profession slew when he first announced the mysteries of the covenant of grace, gave rise to all these ceremonies among the several descendants of Adam. When man by his sin had broken the legal covenant, and so excluded himself from all access to the favorable presence of God, and the tree of life, there was thus a way—"a new and a living way opened up." Jesus was the lamb slain from the foundation of the world. Christ the substitute stood in the gap—he took our sins upon him—he approached the Father, sustaining the majesty of celestial royalty, against which we had rebelled. He approached, althoug he knew he must be smitten with the sword of justice, instead of all those tribes of elect men, whose names he bears on his breast, and in his heart. Verily, " He was wounded for our transgression, he was bruised for our iniquities, the chastisement of our peace was upon him, and by his stripes we are healed. All we like sheep have gone astray, but the Lord hath laid on him the iniquities of us all, says the church. Isa. liii. Abraham saw his day, and was glad. Before Abraham was I AM. It must be very evident to all who know any thing of the burning majesty of the great God, that no mere man in his fallen state can approach this absolute God. His brilliant divinity must be vailed, his burning holiness must be quenched with vicarious blood. He must be approached by a Mediator. Hence Jehovah says by the prophet, "who is this that engaged his heart to approach unto me." Jer. xxx. 21. Surely it can be no other than the Father's equal Son. There is but one God, and one Mediator between God and man, the Man Christ Jesus. He is the Father's equal in his essence and nature, for every son is of the same nature of his father. The son of man is properly man. The Son of God is also really and properly God. In this respect, therefore, he says, I and my Father are one. He condescends, however, not only to wear our nature but also to humble himself to Mediatory servitude. In this nature and character, he says, "My Father is greater than I." John xiv. 28. From another fact, it must appear evident that Abraham could have no intimacy with God, but in and through a Mediator. No man hath seen God at any time, the only begotten who is in the bosom of the Father, he hath declared him. John 1, 18. In and through him God makes a covenant, or ratifies a testimentary deed with all believers. Isa. lv. Incline your ear, and come unto me; hear and your souls shall live, and I will make with you an everlasting covenant, even the sure mercies of David.

There can properly be only two covenants res-

pecting man's happiness in the enjoyment of felicitating fellowship with God. First. A legal covenant with man in innocence. Second. A gracious covenant respecting man in a fallen state.
This cannot be made primarily with man himself.
It must be made with the surety and Mediator of
a better covenant. A covenant have I made with
my *chosen.* Mercy shall be built up for ever.
Psalm lxxxix. This second and better covenant
then, or testament, must be viewed as originally,
& properly made with the Son of God in behalf of
those whom he is graciously to save. It is made
with all believers in the reception of Christ by
faith. They lay hold of the covenant. For Christ
is given a covenant of the people. This latter
covenant of grace, though one in itself, may receive several names, according as it is viewed in
the different steps of its exhibition. As primarily made with Christ for the purpose of buying
back and restoring to liberty the poor captive and
bankrupt man, it may be called the covenant of redemption.—Considering the principle which
moved it, and the character of the divine emana-
tion which it was to communicate, it may be called the covenant of grace. Considering the obligations under which the privileges of this covenant lay covenanters, it may be called a covenant
of duties. personal, ecclesiastical or national, as
the case may be. Considering the final end to
which all leads, and the subserviency of the whole
to the happy result and final close in delivering
the blessed legatees from all evil, and introduc-

ing them into the enjoyment of all good, it may
be called the covenant of salvation.

A right consideration of these facts and principles will assist much in understanding, not only
the term, I will make with you a covenant; but
also to understand the justification of all believers
without the righteousness of the law, and yet the
necessity that faith should not be without works.
It will shew that faith alone justifies, because it
unites its subject the believer with Jesus Christ,
the Lord our righteousness, and yet that faith
does not justify, being alone. It must work by
love, and demonstrate its own genuine nature by
works. From these principles too it will appear
that all negociations with sinful men must be upon
principles of grace and mercy, whether duty is
first exacted, or privilege first announced. No
matter whether "I will be your God, and ye shall
be my people'! or ' believe in the Lord Jesus
Christ and thou shalt be saved."

We reason then thus with respect to the covenant. There is no covenant, whereby God can
be the God of sinful men, but the covenant of
grace; but God by the covenant under consideration became Abraham's God; therefore this was
the covenant of grace.

There is no dispensation whereby any can be
justified but by a dispensation of grace; but A-
braham was justified by this dispensation; therefore this was a dispensation of *grace*. The principle of this is most plain and obvious. By the
works of the law, Truth hath said, no flesh shall

be justified in the sight of God. He hath concluded all under sin. They who believe not the
promises which are all yea and amen in Christ, are
condemned already. But Abraham was justified.
By what law? asks the Apostle ; of works? Nay
but by the law of faith or- dispensation of grace.
Abraham believed God, and it was imputed to
him for righteousness. This same principle was
of general concern in that early period of the
world and of the display of mercy, and so we find
the inspired psalmist in the xxxii Psalm sing of
the blessedness of such characters generally.
" Blessed is the man to whom the Lord imputeth
not his sin." The Apostle Paul quotes this and
reasons from it in proving what we are now proving, viz. *The Grace of the Abrahamic Covenant.*
Rom. iv. 4. Now to him that worketh, i. e.
hath life by the covenant of works is the reward
not reckoned of grace, but of debt. But without
stating and illustrating by fairest syllogism the arguments upon. this topic, let any man read the
chapters of Genesis, in which this patriarch's life
is recorded, and at the same time have in his hand
the epistles of Paul, especially those to the Romans and Galatians, and see unless he has some
favorite system to defend, if he can deny that the
covenant with Abraham was a dispensation of the
covenant of grace. We refer you to those original documents, where you will find this truth not
only stated, but argumentatively proved. It certainly can be no objection against this, that the land
of Canaan was promised to him and his posterity.

For, beside that the land of promise was a typical land, the covenant of grace secures to all believers, that they shall dwell in the land and verily have food. Their place of defence is the munition of rocks, bread shall be given them, and their water shall be sure. With regard to the first of these principles, the Apostle reasons in direct reference to Abraham, and his travelling posterity. " For they that say such things declare plainly that they seek a country ; and truly, if they had been mindful of that country from whence they came out, they might have had an opportunity to have returned. But now they desire a better country, that is an heavenly ; wherefore God is not ashamed to be called *their* God : for he hath prepared for them a city. By what charter did he become *their* God, if not by the covenant of grace ? If it was not by that, it must have been by one as good, for that is all he can become to us. If God is not ashamed to own him as a member of his family below, and an heir of blessedness of the heavenly city above, how arrogant it is, for any to say that this covenant respected nothing more than the land of Canaan ? But again, if the fact that the promise respected their temporary accommodation be admitted ; that cannot militate against its being a dispensation of the covenant of grace, unless you would choose to say that the covenant which is ordered in *all things*, makes no provision for the bodily and temporary wants of God's own people, and is it likely, think you, that Christ has redeemed the bodies of his

D

ransomed ones, and made no provision for their
sustenance? Oh, no. Bread shall be given them;
their water shall be made sure. Though the
lions should be hungry, they shall lack nothing
that is good. To such as seek first the kingdom
of heaven and his righteousness, all other things
shall be added. Whether Paul or Apollos or
Cephas, or the world, all is yours, and ye are
Christ's. Godliness is profitable unto all things,
having the promise of the life that now is, and of
that which is to come. Do these appendages alter the spiritual and everlasting privileges of all
the saints? Do these temporal benefits embraced
in the covenant charter destroy the grace of the
dispensation under which they live? Certainly
not. If these do not destroy the grace of the
covenant with which the faithful generally are fa-
vored, why should they do so in respect of Abraham, the father of the faithful? Oh! I see.
The reason is obvious. If that was the covenant
of grace, then circumcision was its seal, and his
posterity were its subjects. Why should not ours?
Then where goes the plea of the Anabaptist?

Let us next consider the seal of this covenant.

The seal of any covenant is that mark and impress, whereby the parties themselves, and others
may recognise the instrument to be theirs, and
whereby the consent of the covenanters is formally and legally exhibited. It has always been used
by great men, when vouchsafing any particular favour, especially grants of sovereigns to their subjects. Esther iii. 10, 12. When the persons of

the parties are particularly respected in the covenant, the seal is put upon the persons. Esth. viii. 2. Thus the bridegroom betroths or marries the bride by putting on her finger a ring. This is a token of endless attachment—a pledge of mutual possession and permanent kindness in the circle of their intimate union. So the seals of the covenant of grace plight the faith of our divine husband, that he will be ours in an everlasting covenant, on our part we set to, thereby the seal of our consent to his overtures, and persuasion of his truth. We bind ourselves to be constant and chaste in our affection, and punctual and diligent in the observation of his ordinances and statutes. He who is our maker binds himself to be our loving and faithful husband, and we bind ourselves to be his chaste, obedient wife. Circumcision was such a seal, for by it, the Apostle reasons, that men were bound to keep the whole law. It was also the seal of the righteousness of faith.

In times of more patriarchial simplicity and purity, it was not hazardous to discern the mode of this rite's performance.

The times are now too licentiously delicate to admit of such description. We must, therefore, refer the reader to inspired documents, and to ancient histories of Jewish ritual.

It is well known that circumcision was a bloody rite performed upon the generative organ of the male. It alluded, no doubt, to the tragic story of our fall in our first parent, and also to the glorious mystery of godliness, God manifested in

the incarnation and passion of Jesus Christ. The
time of his passing by was a time of love. He
said when we were in our blood ; live. This command could not take effect without satisfaction
paid to divine justice. " Without the shedding
of blood there could be no 'remission." Forasmuch therefore as the children were partakers of
 sh and blood, he himself also took part of the
same, that through death he might destroy death.
Thus, when there was no eye to pity, nor hand to
help, he laid help upon one that was mighty to
save. God sent forth his 'Son to be made of a
woman, made under the law, to redeem them that
were under the law, that we might receive the
adoption of sons. It is no objection to this interpretation that females were not personally subjects. They were considered in and represented
by the males. Had they not been considered of
the circumcision, the Israelitish males in being
forbidden to marry the uncircumcised, would
have been prohibited marriage altogether. Moreover, had this not been the case, it would have
been impossible, according to the carnal, secular
and superficial way in which our opponents consider this rite and seal, for women to be heiresses
of land in the Jewish commonwealth: This was
given to the circumcised and belonged to them,
yet the daughters of Zelophehad who had no
male representatives, could enjoy fast property.

The truth is, females were then, except in a
case of this kind, not known ; they were viewed
either in their fathers or husbands, as their rep-

resentatives. Although it was a sign and a seal of seperation from the natural, and of incision or inoculation into the supernatural stock, it did not effect either of these by any immediate agency. Hence Abraham was a sincere believer before he was circumcised, and no doubt many were converted after this rite had been performed. As the scripture says, He received the sign of circumcision, "A *seal* of the righteousness of the faith which he had, yet being uncircumcised." Rom. iv. 11. So closely, however, was the *seal* connected with the *covenant*, that the one is sometimes put for the other. Gen. xvii. 10. "This is my covenant which ye shall keep between me and you, and thy seed after thee : Every man child among you shall be circumcised." It is explained in the next verse—"and it shall be a token between me and you, and he that is eight days old shall be circumcised among you, every man child in your generations.—And my covenant shall be in your flesh for an everlasting covenant." The subjects of this ordinance were adult descendants of Abraham and their infant male seed; proselytes and their male offspring. Nay, not only their immediate descendants, but all of their households of whose education they had a charge. v. 23, 24, 25, 26.—And all the men of his house, born in the house; and bought with money of the stranger, were circumcised, &c. chap. xviii. 19. For I know him, that he will command his children and household after him; and they shall keep the way of the Lord.

The great promise of this covenant we have already in part considered. "And I will be their God." It is evident that this embraces every thing. They are a blessed people whose God is Jehovah. It must embrace immortality, for God is not the God of the dead, but of the living. It is trifling to say that according to this reasoning all the circumcised would necessarily be saved. Try this reasoning with relation to baptism as administered upon any subject and in any mode. Circumcision only profited when the thing signified was by grace present. Circumcision verily profiteth, if thou keep the law, if otherwise, circumcision became uncircumcision. Those who had been circumcised in infancy, and acted according to that vow, fulfilled the moral and religious rites, to which they were by that early honour and privilege bound. It was profitable to them. They were visibly in covenant with God, and had a right, of course, to the fellowship of the Church; if otherwise, they lost their right to this gracious promise. I will be your God. This promise is evidently a running or current promise. I *will* be their God. Are there any who may now claim an interest in this covenant promise? Under what covenant are they? Doubtless under the covenant of Grace. But why should not Abraham be considered under that same covenant of grace, unto whom this promise was first given? Its permanency is also evinced from the extent of its application. Gen. xvii. 3,4. And Abram fell on his face; and God talked with him saying, as for me, behold my covenant is with thee, and thou shalt be a father of *many nations*. Can we limit this expression to the nation of the Jews? Certainly not. Nay, it contemplates the good of all nations in a future day, for he has promised who will perform, " I *will* bless them that bless thee ; and curse him that curseth thee, and in thee shall *all* families of the earth be blessed. It is admitted that many received privileges, both temporal and spiritual, by becoming citizens of the Jewish common-wealth and members of the Church. These were proselytes of the gate and proselytes of the covenant. It will also be granted that some who were friendly towards them, received favours on that account. Instance Hiram, Bibler, Hur, Josephus, &c. But this promise seems to imply something more. That they even *all* the *families* of the earth, should be blessed in him. But how, it will be asked, in him? It will be granted that those who descended legally and naturally from him, had many advantages. They were in him seminally—he was their natural parent—they were in him, when the promise was given—they had a primary interest in this covenant. Hence, when Cephas preached and baptised, he performed this his ministry among the descendants of Abraham in the wilderness of Judea. Christ preached to them almost exclusively. From them he called his disciples—he commands them to go only to the lost sheep of the house of Israel. Although the inhabitants of Samaria called Jacob their father, and said our fathers worshipped in this mountain, yet our Saviour knew they were mongrels and aliens from the commonwealth of Israel, and so he says to his disciples—"Into the cities of Samaria enter not." " It is not meet to take the children's meat and cast it to dogs. He calls them emphatically his own. John 1. He came unto his own. Though they are now under sore judgments for rejecting and crucifying their Messiah, yet they are still preserved a distinct people for singular blessings in the latter days, according to the covenant which sovereignly manifests such favors for the descendants of Abraham. 2d. *In* him respects the descent of Christ from him. Whose are the fathers and of whom as concerning the flesh, Christ came, who is God over all, blessed forever. Rom. ix. 5. Not as though the word of God had taken none effect. For they are not all Israel which are of Israel : but, in Isaac shall thy seed be called ; that is, they which are the children of the flesh, these are not the children of God : but the children of the promise are counted for the seed. This is quoted and argued from Gen. xxi. 12, where Abraham is comforted upon the expulsion of Hagar's son from before the face of Sarah. The Apostle reasons on the same topic, and to the same amount in his epistle to the Galatians. iii. 16. Now to Abraham and to his *seed* were the promises made. He saith not to seeds, as of many ; but as of one; and to thy *seed,* which is Christ. The Son of God by incarnation was clothed with human nature, and that in an eminent sense from Abraham, as the first noted character, from whom he should directly spring. For verily he took not on him the nature of angels ; but he took on him the seed of Abraham. Heb. ii. 16. This may seem hard to reconcile with what has before been quoted. How is he the seed and yet takes on him the seed ? He *is* the seed when he takes his name from his humanity. He takes the seed when he is denominated from his divinity. This will receive illustration, if we attend to what is said of Christ and David in relation to each other. Says Christ, " I am the *root* and the *offspring* of David. He was David's root as God—David's offspring as man. So also, though before Abraham in his divine nature, He was in him and from him as man. 3d. *In thee* or in thy seed respects his spiritual descendants. " Say not, we have Abraham to our Father, for God is able of these stones to raise up seed to Abraham." All then are the children of Abraham who are believers, heirs of his faith. But how are they his children or seed, if he and they do not believe substantially the same promises, and be interested in the same covenant ? Are not believers now heirs of the covenant of promise or of grace ? Is not this the same as being heirs of his faith ? If this be the case, then either they are not in the covenant of grace, or he was. If he was, then the Abrahamic covenant was a dispensation of the covenant of grace. But his posterity, even when infants, were visibly admitted into the same external privileges, and had, until they forfeited the right; an interest in the blessing of God being their God. Why should not this be the case still? the reflecting reader will ask. We leave the answer to those who oppose infant baptism. It is evident that believers and their seed have now the same essential privileges that Abraham had. Had he God for his God? was he an heir of God by the promise? So are we. Those who rejected the promise of the Saviour are for a while rejected. We are in their room admitted into the number and have a right to all the privileges of the sons of God. John 1; 12. As many as received him; to them gave he power to become the sons of God, even to them that believe on his name. No matter whether they are descended of him or not, if they are in the same covenant by regeneration. Who are born not of blood, or of the will of the flesh, or of the will of man, but of God. He is no longer exclusively the God of the Jews, or natural descendants of Abraham. No, the covenant charter continues the same in its internal and essential benefits; is become far more liberal in its exhibition; more inward and spiritual in its application. " Is he the God of the Jews only? is he not of the Gentiles also? yes of the Gentiles also." Rom. iii. 29. Has the Jew then no advantage? Yes; because to them was the covenant of promise or grace first given. They had a precedency in the order of succession; but we a pre-eminence in the nature of the dispensation. Many of the Fathers and righteous men desired to see the days which we see. For though they had the promise given, they received not what it very emphatically contemplated. But it is evident their dispensation was of grace or promise notwithstanding. The covenant of grace was the same, its dispensation was different. To them it was dispensed by promises, prophecies, circumcision and the passover, which were for the time, by the same spirit of God which is now necessary, sufficient for the salvation of all whom God designed to save. Now when Christ the substance is exhibited, the same covenant of grace is exhibited by preaching the word, and administering the sacraments with more fullness, evidence and efficacy to all nations. If this view, which reforming divines have always taken of this subject, be not correct, and the view which the Anabaptist takes be correct, then was Abraham, and were the ancient believers and saints of the Old Testament saved at all? By whom? By Christ, who is the same yesterday, to-day and forever. There is no other name given under heaven whereby men can be saved. But by what covenant did Christ become their Saviour? We call that the covenant of grace whereby Christ and salvation are graciously communicated unto men, however the mode of dispensation may circumstantially vary. If our opponents then agree about this fundamental point, we will think we have gained something of importance. If not, then how were they honored and privileged by the revelations given them. Might not the same external favors been granted without the formality of a covenant at all? If not, what are we to think of the Apostle's reasoning? Without faith it is impossible to please God. But how could they believe in him, of whom they had not yet heard? and how can they hear without a preacher? as it is written, how beautiful are the feet of them that bring glad tidings, or preach the gospel! From all this then it would seem they had the covenant of grace, and the gospel, or they could not believe. If this were not the case, how could believers all unite in a song to *Him* that washed them from their sins, and redeemed them out of every kindred and place and nation? Is Abraham and the saints of venerable story to be mute when this celestial exercise is felicitating the hearts of others? No; to him and to them the gospel was preached. Further, let us consider the Abrahamic covenant, as it affected the social state of his posterity, and that of his Gentile believing descendants. Sometimes this is compared to a vine or tree, sometimes to a city or corporation, sometimes to a nation or community.

Thou hast brought a vine out of Egypt. Psalm lxxx. 8. Trees may undergo a great many incidental changes, and yet continue the same. They may shed fruit, cast leaves, increase vastly in size by the process of vegetation; may lose branches by the pruning-hook, may receive new branches by ingrafting. So long as the stock remains, the tree is the same. Thus the visible society of God's people is represented as still the same vine, even in the days of David, notwithstanding the many years and revolutions which had taken place while the Church was in the wilderness, in the time of the judges, and of his predecessor Saul. Yea, after the captivity they are still viewed as the same society, although during that time the cities had been laid waste without inhabitants, and the houses without men, and the land desolate. But yet in it shall be a tenth, and it shall return and shall be eaten ; as a teil tree and as an oak whose substance is in them, when they cast their leaves, so the holy seed shall be the substance thereof. Isa. vi. 13.

Now what was it that maintained the identity of this plant ? It was the holy seed, It had not only the organization of a plant by the covenant charter, but it had also a substance from the spirit, of Jesus Christ, who is the same yesterday, to-day and forever. Thus he speaks of the same subject in the New-Testament. John xv. 1. I am the true vine, and my Father is the husbandman. Every branch in me that beareth not fruit, he taketh away : and every branch that beareth fruit he purgeth it that it may bring forth more fruit. From this passage it is evident that there are two ways of being in Christ, viz. one by profession of religion, and another by possession of real grace. The former the great husbandman taketh away. This he does in several ways. By discipline when faithfully administered by the servants of God and stewards of his house, those who bear no fruit, or bad fruit, will be taken away. The

E

laborers will cut off the dry branches by the au.
thority of the great Husbandman. By perseeu-
tion or some worldly inconvenience, those who
hold not religion in supreme consideration, will
be tempted to part with it. When the profession
of the truth requires sacrifice—anon they are of-
fended—they went out from us, i. e. from our
visible connection, because they were not of us,
i. e. by inward, spiritual union. Sometimes this
may be omitted, till death make the final separation, when the tares resemble very much the
wheat ;—the taking of the tares may be postponed
until the wheat is ripe, and then the wheat will be
gathered into the heavenly granary, and the tares
will be cast into the unquenchable fire of hell.
Those who, like the rich man in the parable, do
nothing for God's poor chuich and people, but
think themselves bound to do nothing more than
what the laws of the community bind them to do,
will then see their mistake, when the Lazaruses
whom they have neglected, shall be in Abraham's
bosom, and they rejected, and not a drop of water
be afforded to cool their scorching tongues.

This subject will receive farther illustration, if
we attend to the Apostle's reasoning. Rom. xi.
He asks—Hath God cast away his people? God
forbid! For I also am an Israelite of the seed of
Abraham, of the tribe of Benjamin. He shews
that there was an election or remnant of the body
of Israel, even at that time, when the multitude
were unbelieving and so evidently going to destruction. He seems to hint too that there were

more of these than perhaps some superficial ob-
servers would reckon. In times of prosperity in
the Church, there seems to be more than they really are ; in times of persecution and of Sion's
trouble, there will appear to be fewer than they
really are. This he illustrates from the state of
the church in Elijah's time. When the prophet
concluded that he was alone, God told him he had
reserved seven thousand in Israel who had not
bowed the knee to the image of Baal. Seven
thousand who had walked in the holy way of their
father Abraham, who, with his posterity, were to
be seperated, by profession and practice, from the
idolatrous nations was a considerable number, and
yet it was nothing to the many thousands of Israel who followed the popular and court religion
of that very corrupt time. The Apostle accordingly says—"Even so then at this present time,
there is a remnant according to the election of
grace." This small remnant however are more
counted of than all the rest, although a very in-
considerable minority. They have the ecclesiastical constitution upon their side. Accordingly
the rest are represented as branches broken off;
they are spoken of as the original stock. v. 17.
And if some of the branches be broken off, and
thou being a wild olive tree, wert grafted in a-
mong them, and with them partakest of the root
and fatness of the olive tree, boast not against the
branches : but if thou boast, thou bearest not the
root but the root thee. What then is this good
olive tree from which some branches were lopped

and into which some others were engrafted ?
It is evident it must be a church state ; for about
church matters he is reasoning. Whether then
is it about a church state of ancient or of modern
organization ? of Jewish or of Gentile origin ? or
to speak in the ordinary way about this subject,
does the Apostle mean by this good olive tree
the Jewish or the Christian Church ? It is evident it cannot be the latter, for the Jews as such
never belonged to this organization ; of course
could not be taken off that on which they never
were fixed. The Apostle considers however the
Church constitution essentially one. There is
but one Church. It is quite absurd to speak of a
Jewish and a Christian church, for the same
church which was in the wilderness, is now and
ever will be. The mountains may depart, and
the hills be removed, but the covenant of his peace,
eminently revealed to Abraham, renewed with
Isaac and Jacob, shall never be removed. I would
not have you ignorant, says the Apostle, that all
our fathers were under the cloud, and all passed
through the sea, and were all baptised unto Moses
in the cloud & in the sea ; and did all eat the same
spiritual meat, and did all drink the same spiritual drink ; for they drank of the rock that followed them, and that rock was Christ. 1 Cor. x. 1,
2, 3, 4. The Saviour and spiritual things were
known to them by different names, and exhibited
in different modes, but these spiritual things are
still the same.—The Saviour still one and the
same. There are diversities of administration,

but the same spirit. Were the Gentiles now introduced into gracious privileges and blessings of the covenant of grace in a church state? Well. It was the same blessing and the same covenant state which Abraham before enjoyed, and into which his posterity were through him introduced. Thus the Apostle reasons. Gal. iii. 14. That the blessing of Abraham might come on the Gentiles through Jesus Christ; that we might receive the promise of the Spirit through faith. v. 15. Brethren, I speak after the manner of men; Though it be but a man's covenant; (does not this most clearly shew that the covenant he speaks of is God's covenant, or the covenant of grace, for he reasons from the less to the greater) yet if it be confirmed, no man disannulleth, or addeth thereto. v. 16. Now to Abraham and his seed were the promises made. All this is so congenial not only with the tenor and scope of scripture, but even with the honest and fair negociations of men in a social state, according to the representative system, that it may indeed seem strange that any should either deny or misunderstand it. Sure every one knows that so long as the charter of any society continues, or the constitution of any community, that it is still the same society, and the same community, although it may change a thousand times its members; be increased or diminished, or altered in its by laws to any degree you can imagine. Suppose a civil society to be formed by settling at first all of one nation, it is afterwards mixed, and finally the descendants of

the original stock become extinct—it is still the
same political body.   All the treaties or contracts
made by the aborigines would stand in the court
of nations, and the original constitution would
just as much belong to the last members as to the
first.   This principle of the identity of organic
bodies, seems to be understood in physics and
ethics, and jurisprudence—in every thing but
where it is most true and of most importance that
is in regard of the Church.

What privileges do we Gentiles now enjoy ?
Is it not that though once aliens, we are now fellow citizens, and of the household of faith ? We
are come, not to the mount that might be touch-
ed, and that burned with fire and to blackness and
darkness, or we are not introduced into the dark,
typical, and terrific legal part of ancient dispensations.   But we are come to mount Sion and unto
the city of the living God, to the heavenly Jerusalem, and to an innumerable company, of angels.
To the general assembly and *Church* of the *first*
born which are written in heaven, and to God the
judge of all, and to the spirits of just men made
perfect.

Were God's people as a nation called out of
and separated from an unbelieving idolatrous
world ? So are we—called out of every people
and tongue and nation, to be to him a peculiar
people, a holy nation, a royal priesthood. But
are we by this made a new society or different
community from that which God of old redeemed ? He has but one body, for he is one head;

he has one sheep-fold, for he is one shepherd ;
one kingdom ; 'for he is one king. By the blood
of the covenant he·has made of twain 'one new
man, so making, peace. 'In Christ there is neither Jew nor Gentile, bond nor'free : all are one,
He has united all things in heaven or in earth.
Is this done by altering the constitution and arrangement of .things respecting those already in
glory, or is it not rather by altering and conforming things on earth to the pattern of things in
heaven ? Either then the ancient saints were
trained up for that place, by a dispensation of
grace, or we are not, or they and we cannot be
united. If they were not, and we are, then our education and theirs are essentially different. 'They
and we are not, cannot, be socially and beatifically
united. One will speak the language of Canaan,
and the other the language of Ashdod. 'They
will be barbarians to us, and we to them. We
cannot be united as one nation, our language, our
sentiments, our spirit' have been so different.
Who but sees the absurdity of this ? They without us could not be perfect, nor we without them.
The reason is obvious. The body is one. 'We
are all members one of another. All must be
unitedly exhibited as the reward of his-suffering,
when he shall see of the travail of his soul, and be
satisfied ; when he shall surrender the ·kingdom
unto his father ; saying here am I. and·the children whom thou hast given me. Though ·gath-
ered from different ages and places', they shall
then be ONE GREAT NATION. The· charter ·has

always been the same. The one charter of all their rights has been the covenant of grace, and when all the diversities of opinions shall be dispelled, by the vision of glory, the differences of times, in which they have lived, shall be all lost in the duration of eternity. Then shall Abel, the Protomartyr, whose spirit first of human souls, enjoyed celestial bliss, and the last believing spirit, who shall close up the rear of the great ransomed multitude, unite in sweetest symphony, in shouting, "Grace, Grace, unto it."

But are we still told that this all might be the case, and yet the Abrahamic covenant not be a dispensation of the covenant of grace, because he lived in a typical period? What!' might grace be exhibited, and grace applied for salvation, and yet the dispensation not be gracious? It must be remembered that typical and gracious are not opposites, capable of being contrasted, or contradictory, incapable of reconciliation. Of what were the ordinances of that period typical? Do you say, of the external ordinances of the gospel dispensation? Then there must be some antitype in these of the rite of initiation. What is that, if not baptism? Again do you say, they were typical of spiritual things? If so, then what is the essential difference between them and the ordinances of grace now? In this sense the ordinances may still be called typical, for they still address men's reason through the organs of sense and perception. They yet regard man as consisting of soul and body; a candidate in time for eternity.

Is it farther objected, that our system makes Abraham a Mediator? We answer, by no means. On the contrary, we establish from scripture that he had the same *One* Mediator that all believers have. The covenant we have seen was not originally made with him. It was the eternal covenant which only received a formal and eminent ratification with this illustrious patriarch. Finally. Is it objected that nothing but a natural birth was required in the Abrahamic covenant, but that a spiritual birth is necessary in order to partake of the privileges of the covenant of grace?

To this we answer, by asking; Were there any saved under that dispensation? Were the believers of that day, and under that dispensation regenerated or unregenerated? Did they believe without the operation of the Spirit, or with it? If with it, then they were regenerated, as well as we. If they were not, how did they enter into heaven? Except a man be born again he cannot enter into the kingdom of heaven. Is it said the kingdom in John iii. means the visible Church? Grant it, and are the terms of admittance into the latter stricter than into the former? Can they be admitted into the heavenly society without regeneration, and not into the earthly—into the triumphant, and not into the militant Church!!!

Again, can none be members of the church now unless they be regenerate? Was Judas regenerated? No; he was the son of perdition. Was Simon the sorcerer regenerated? No; he was in the gall of bitterness and in the bond of iniquity. Were the stony ground hearers, the tares and the many that shall say, Lord, Lord, &c. at the last suing for admittance renewed? Were they who fled for fear of persecution, regenerated, who went out from us, because they were not of us? These descriptions were all privileged with the participation of gospel ordinances; belonged to the visible society of the saints, yet unregenerate.

The truth on this subject appears to be this, that the Church in old and new testament times, has had true and false members. The true members always were made so by the regeneration of the Holy Spirit. This benefit is certainly implied, and, that not obscurely, in the great promise of this dispensation. I will be your God. This the apostle Peter quotes to encourage his 3000 converts. " The promise," says he "is to you and to your children." This he mentions to encourage them that they should receive the Holy Ghost. It is then evident that if a dispensation, whereby God is manifested in mercy through Jesus Christ, and by the Spirit of God be a dispensation of grace, this covenant with Abraham must be so called, i. e. *The Abrahamic covenant was gracious.* Not only has it continued to unfold its stores of grace to all ages past, but will in all ages of time and eternity to come.

I will be your God. It intimated that all the several advances of the covenants execution, would take place in their proper order and time ; of course, that Christ would appear as the great *seed*—that he would be cut off, but not for him-

self, that he would bring in an everlasting righteousness, Dan ix. 24, that in him, all nations, of
the earth should finally be blessed.

Hence it is evident that a great many blessings
of this covenant are yet to be enjoyed. We
are not without our interest in it, if we be believers, God is our God, and the God of our
seed, as well as he was the God of Abraham and
his. We reckon that he is so by the greatest
grace. This promise will be eminently accom-
plished, when the Jews shall be brought in by
the fulness of the Gentiles. All Israel shall be
saved, as it is written, Isaiah lix. 20. " And
the Redeemer shall come to Zion, and unto them
that turn from transgression in Jacob, saith the
Lord. As for me, *this is my covenant* with them,
saith the Lord ; My Spirit that is upon thee and
my words which I have put into thy mouth,
shall not depart out of thy mouth ; nor out of
the mouth of thy seed, nor out of the mouth of
thy seed's seed, saith the Lord, from henceforth
and forever. Then shall men be particularly
blessed in the seed of Abraham ; all nations
shall call him blessed, according to the promise
of this gracious covenant. The people shall
praise him, all the people shall praise him : The
earth shall yield its increase, and God, even *our*
God, shall bless us. Whereas, but a small people, inhabiting a little spot of territory, were anciently his peculiar possession, then shall the
kingdoms of the world, become the kingdoms of
our Lord, and of his Christ. This great do-

minion shall extend from sea to sea, and from
the river unto the ends of the earth. The
whole world shall be filled with the knowledge of the glory of the Lord. One shall say,
I am the Lord's, and another shall subscribe himself by the name of Jacob; and another shall
subscribe with his hand unto the Lord, and
surname himself by the name of Israel. They
shall say, come and let us join ourselves unto the
Lord, in an everlasting covenant that shall not be
forgotten. But even in all the glories, and felicity of the millenial age, we shall not exhaust the
blessings and grace of this covenant. *" I will be
your God,* no, they shall come from the east, and
from the west, and sit down *with* Abraham and
Isaac and Jacob, in the kingdom of our heavenly
Father. They shall encircle, according to this
charter, the Eternal's throne. They shall inhab-
it those mansions, which the Redeeming Seed
hath purchased, prepared, and preoccupied.
Then all the ransomed of the Lord, shall meet
on the summit of the heavenly Sion, and join in
the harmonious choir of praise to God and the
Lamb, in the new Jerusalem, for ever and ever.

PART III.

The permanent sanction of the moral Law.

IT is very observeable that in all the dispensations of Providence, and grace, the young and helpless are preserved and defended. Among the animal tribes, the operations of providential kindness to this effect, are very conspicuous. By the storgeal affection and parental instinct their indigent and imbecile young are nourished, with unwearied kindness, and defended sometimes by fraud, sometimes by force, with astonishing skill, and courage. The weak seem to say, I am strong ; and the timid who have recourse to no defence for themselves, but flight, will, when guarding their young, place themselves in belligerent attitude, against the fiercest assailant, and most rapacious destroyer.

To this interesting phenomenon, God's care of his people, and children, is often compared. In the period of Israel's redemption, and the subsequent Sinaic legislation, God's care for the seed of Israel, and the children of his people, is remarkable.

The Egyptian policy, worse than savage cruelty, contemplated the diminution of Israel's strength.—Every male infant, for this purpose, must be put to death. But no, the matrons of

F

Israel are strong, and the midwives of Egypt are
tender. The children are spared ; the more they
are oppressed, the more they grow—they come
out not one week among all their tribes. The
Egyptians are caught in their own net—their
prime youth are cut off—the Lord of hosts saves
one and rears him up in the Egyptian palace, who
is to deliver Israel's sons. " The children of
Israel sighed by reason of the bondage. And
God heard their groaning, and God remembered
his covenant with Abraham, with Isaac and with
Jacob." Those who were saved from the waters
of the river, sing an epinikeon over their enemies
immersed in the depths of the sea.

In that deliverance the future good of the infants of Abraham's posterity, is particularly con-
sulted. The adults thus redeemed, with the exception of two, fall in the wilderness.

When he brought this ransomed family out of
the iron furnace, he would not lead them through
the populous region which lay along the shore of
the Mediterranean, but led them through the de-
vious wilds of Arabia Petrea. This he did, partly because he knew their hearts were tender, they
might be afraid of military force by the way ;
partly that he might teach them, in early life, the
knowledge of his covenant and law. They were,
as a nation, just in early infancy ; unfit yet to act
for themselves, yet were they very obviously re-
garded by God's covenant, and so must be matriculated in his school, that they might be educated, as those who were heirs of a heavenly

Canaan, and candidates of an incorruptible inheritance. " And God said moreover unto Moses: Thus shalt thou say unto the *children* of Israel. The Lord God of your fathers, the God of Abraham, the God of Isaac, and the God of Jacob hath sent me unto you. This is my name forever, and this is my memorial unto all generations." He will be known by a name expressive of his relation to this patriarch and his seed forever. Of his gracious kindness according to his covenant, to the posterity of Abraham, he will preserve a memorial to all generations of men.

That this legislative transaction should disannul the covenant of promise is very unlikely. That it should, there can hardly be supposed any thing more absurd, unless it should be, that the anti-typical redemption did. " Is the law then against the promise of God ? God forbid ; for if there had been a law which could have given life, verily righteousness should have been by the law." Gal. iii. 21.

It is not only upon the principles of priority, which in all courts is a strong claim, but also because both of these events were contemplated in this ancient covenant. We have seen that the redemption from Egypt was effected by the Lord, because he remembered his covenant with their fathers, and it is equally evident that the New-Testament redemption of his people out of all nations, wherein they have been servants of sin and slaves to Satan, is contemplated in the very terms of the Abrahamic dispensation of the covenant of grace. Gal. iii. 8. " And the scripture foreseeing that God would justify the heathen through faith, preached the gospel before unto Abraham, saying, In thee shall all nations be blessed: So then they which be of faith are blessed with faithful Abraham. v. 17. And this I say, that the covenant that was confirmed before of God in Christ, the law that was 430 years after, cannot disannul that it should make the promise of none effect." It is true, if the law should be considered as a covenant of works, and obedience to it be the supposed condition of life and happiness, then it would have this effect, to abrogate the previous dispensation of grace. But this was not the case. v 13. " For if the inheritance be of the law, it is no more of promise, but God gave it to Abraham by promise. The moral law however was and still is useful. By this sinners are led to the knowledge of sin, and believers are directed to duty. It is a rule of life in the hands of a Mediator to believers.

The ceremonial law was a veiled gospel, or as the scripture expresses it, a schoolmaster to bring us to Christ, that we might be justified by faith. So far from Christ's coming to destroy the ancient covenant of promise, that the promises were in him, all yea and amen. They were fulfilled and ratified in Jesus Christ. In the giving of the law and the redemption of that period, he is known by the name Jehovah, immutable in his character, and faithful to his promises of salvation. Then might Israel say, " The Lord is our judge, the Lord is our lawgiver, the Lord is our king, he will save us." The intelligent would at once see that the law was holy, and just, and good.

It is evident too, that whatever were the manifestations of propitious providence and benign grace to adults ; the same, if not greater, were made to the children. They, as well as the adults, "are baptised in the cloud and in the sea." God carries them as on eagles wings—he spreads his cloudy presence over them, to correct the fervid heat of day, and chilling damps of night. To all of them in the preface of this law, he most graciously says. " I am the Lord your God." The form of this preface, as well as its place in relation to the law, will abundantly satisfy all who know any thing about grace, that there was grace in this legation, and, so long as grace shall last, this law must of course be considered as having a *gracious sanction*. " Because God is the Lord and our God and Redeemer, therefore we are bound to keep all his commandments."

I. is true the trumpet of the Almighty sounded long and strong : in peals of hoarse thunder the Eternal gave his voice ; but still it was the voice of the everlasting Father inculcating salutary precepts and maxims upon his children. He claims them all as his. Ex. xii. 1, 2. " And the Lord spake unto Moses, saying, Sanctify unto me all the first born ;" and as the Apostle reasons, " If the first fruits be holy, the lump is also holy, if the root be holy, so are the branches." Particular provision was made for the education of youth in this code. v. 8th. " And thou shalt show thy son in that day, saying ; This is done because of that which the Lord did unto me, when I came forth out of Egypt. v. 9. And it shall be for a sign unto thee upon thine hand, and for a memorial between thine eyes ; that the *Lord's law* may be in thy mouth, for with a strong hand hath the Lord brought thee out of Egypt." v. 14. And it shall be, when thy son asketh thee in time to come, saying. What is this ? that thou shalt say unto him, By strength of hand the Lord brought us out from Egypt, from the house of bondage." There was gospel mystery in all these rites and in the events which they commemorated, and therefore the parents must be careful to instruct their children in their allusion and signification. They were charged not only to answer the questions, which juvenile curiosity might propound, and which parental piety will always feel a peculiar pleasure to gratify ; but they were to make the gospel of their time and of that dispensation the great topic of discourse !

Children were embraced and contemplated in the body of the decalogue or ten commandments. Thus in the second, parents are charged by all the solicitude they would naturally have for their children, to worship God in no other way than in that of divine institution. They must make to themselves no similitude or imitation for their supposed help or imaginary gratification in worship. They must receive, observe and keep pure and entire all such religious worship and ordinan-

ces as God hath appointed in his word. Why?
"For I the Lord thy God am a jealous God, visiting the iniquities of the fathers upon the children unto the third and fourth generation of them
that hate me, and shewing mercy unto thousands
of them that love me and keep my commandments." See how abundant he is in mercy and
grace even in legislation.

Again, in the fourth precept of the decalogue,
where he enjoins the sanctification of one whole
day in seven, he enacts that all the holy man's
household shall partake of this rest. The seventh
day is the sabbath of the Lord *thy God*; in it,
thou shalt not do any work, thou nor thy son, nor
thy daughter, nor thy man servant, nor thy maid
servant, nor thy cattle, nor the stranger that is
within thy gates; for in six days the *Lord* made
heaven and earth, &c. The same character who
is before called their God, in reference to covenant relation, is here said to be the Lord that
made heaven and earth; wherefore it s evident,
that if any have another God than the God of A-
braham, and of Israel as their God, he is not the
Lord that made all things. In the fifth commandment too, the covenant relation of God to
his people in all successive generations is very
obvious. "Honor thy father and thy mother,
that thy days may be long in the land, which the
Lord *thy God* g veth thee." This commandment is quoted in the New Testament, as a part
of a code, by which it is evident the whole of that
code is sanctioned.

Would any intelligent lawyer quote from a
volume of laws which had been publicly repealed? It is evident therefore, that when the Apostle said, Eph. vi. 2. "Honor thy father and mother (which is the first commandment with promise) it was not known that this law was repealed.
It does not appear indeed that any, who believed
the scriptures, doubted the *sanction of the Moral
Law.*

As the blessing of God was to be upon their
basket and their store in their observation of
those laws, it is evident that every successive
generation were profited by that law, if they kept
it, and no law is accountable for the inconven-
iences which accrue from its violation. Indeed
the more there are, the stronger its authority.
If this law was good for one generation, it would
be good for all generations; so long as mankind
continue the same, and in so far as circumstances
are similar. The influence of example is great,
upon society, when that is good it must be very
beneficial. The example, which the observance
of this law would exhibit, would, from generation
to generation, be salutary and beneficent.

In the re-exhibition of the law given in the
book of Deuteronomy; which signifies the second
law; or second edition of the law; the same principle of gracious attention to children is still observed. This second promulgation of the law
took place about forty years after the first; for
although the distance is but about 200 miles from
Horeb to Kadesh they spent about 40 years in

travelling it. Their lust, their unbelieving fears
caused this long delay in the wilderness. When
they were rightly in their senses, they acknowledged that the system of rule given to them from
Moses, was, wholesome and good. Deut. 1, 14.
"And he answered and said, the thing which
thou hast spoken is good for us to do." They
had anticipated great danger, but contrary to
their unbelieving fears, their children were introduced safe under the auspicies of their heavenly
Father, gracious Protector and divine Redeemer. v. 39. "Moreover your little ones which ye
said should be a prey, and your children which in
that day had no knowledge between good and
evil, they shall go in hither, and unto them will I
give it, and they shall possess it."

The history of the renovation of this covenant
is given in the xxix chap. "These are the words
of the covenant which the Lord commanded Moses to make with the children of Israel in the
land of Moab, beside the covenant which he made
with them in Horeb. v. 10. Ye stand all of you
before the Lord your God, your captains of your
tribes, your elders and your officers. v. 11. Your
little-ones !" Not only those who were there
born, but also those who were not-born were considered by representation present. v. "That
thou shouldest enter into covenant with the Lord
thy God, and into his oath which the Lord thy
God maketh with thee this day ; that he may establish thee to day for a people unto himself, and
that he may be unto thee a God as he said unto

thee, and as he hath swore unto thy fathers, to
Abraham, to Isaac and to Jacob. Neither with
you only do I make this covenant and this oath;
but with him that standeth with us this day before the Lord our God, and *also with him that is*
not here this day. v. 29. Those things which are
revealed, belong unto us and to our *children* forever, that we may do all the works of this law."

From all these facts respecting the utility of
the law in its nature and tendency, and from its
durability in its very form, it must be evident, that,
if these moral and salutary precepts be abrogated,
their abrogation must be very explicit, and must
be done by competent authority.

It sometimes happens that people through prejudice, pride, and superstition, are attached to
systems which they had better renounce; but it
is also true, that a great deal depends upon the
attachment of a people to a system, whether it
shall be salutary to them or not. To this we
may, with safety add, that it is very improbable,
to say the least of it, that a people would be too
much attached to the laws of their God. Were
the children of Israel ever blamed for this? No.
They are blamed for the very contrary. They
made void the law of God through their traditions. Whatever therefore Christ and his Apostles say against the Pharisees, Scribes, and Law-
givers of that period, must be understood against
their traditionary expositions, and superstitious
observances of human appendages; not against
the law itself. It is true they might put too much,

dependance on the literal observance of the law.
The law is only good when lawfully used, and
Doctors of law have still an adage, "Summum
jus est summa injuria." The height of the law
is the height of injustice. They abused the law
very much, by taking those precepts which were
designed to regulate the decisions of the judge
upon the bench, in times when greatest rigour
was necessary, these they took to be common
maxims, of ordinary life. By this means they
justified their relentless cruelty and revengeful
disposition. The law was not to blame for this ;
nor is Christ to be considered as speaking against
the law of retaliation in every case when he reproves this its abuse. Neither will the reproof
which he administers to profane swearers be considered, by any but ignorant enthusiasts or designing knaves, to be a repeal of the law respecting testimony upon oath. " An oath for confir-
-mation is still an ordinance of God to put an end
to strife."

Judicious and tender Christians may, and still
do, testify against cruelties perpetrated by individuals and communities under the pretext of laws
even divine. They may, and still do, testify a-
gainst the profane forms, and profane frequency
of oaths. They, notwithstanding, constantly
plead that individuals, Churches and nations
should avouch God to be their God—that they
should walk in his statutes, keep his ordinances,
and in case of sufficient importance and difficulty
swear by his great and dreadful name.

If this be considered digression, we are not to
blame, but our opponents, who have dragged it
into the controversy. If they are forced to take
refuge in an antinomian plea, it cannot be against
the law or cause of this controversy to plead for
the *permanent sanction of the Moral Law.* I
know some of the baptist brethren will say, We
do not affirm that Christ came to destroy the law.
We do say with the Apostle—" The law is holy
and just and good. We wish they would all say
so. When they do, we shall in our negociations
with them, desist from long discussions of a con-
troversial nature on this point. It is extremely
difficult at present for their want of union among
themselves to know, in what manner to meet them
on their views of the law. They have encompassed the camp of truth; not in regular battalions
marching in rank and file, but in skulking parties,
like companies of Indians, hordes of Vandals, or
legions of Gog and Magog. Some say there are
ten commandments; some say there are eleven;
some say there are six; some four; some two;
some one; some none. Some say there are ten,
but like the Papists who, erasing the second, because it does not well comport with their hosts
and images, make two of the tenth. So some of
the modern Reformers take away the fourth and
supply the law of love in its room. Love, to
be sure is of great moment, both in morals and religion, but it is also very evident that it is rather
a compound or summary of the whole law than a
distinct precept of itself. Love is the fulfilling of

the law. All the law, i. e. of relative duty, is comprehended in this :—"thou shalt love thy neighbor as thyself."

"Thou shalt love the Lord thy God with all thy heart, with all thy soul, with all thy strength, and with all thy mind; this is the first and great commandment, and the second is like unto it, thou shalt love thy neighbor as thyself. On these two hang all the law and the prophets" In the degraded state of morals which prevailed in the time of Christ, when relative and religious duties were made to consist in hollow forms, there was an obvious propriety of enforcing, with special emphasis, the great moral and spiritual essence of the law, which is love.

In the New Testament there was no need to give a ceremonial code of law. That was already done in the ancient legislation. To this system our great Lord, Judge and Lawgiver constantly referred. When the young man in a legal spirit asked, saying, Good Master, what good thing shall I do that I may have eternal life, Matthew xix. 11. And he said unto him, Why callest thou me good? there is none good but one, that is God; but if thou wilt enter into life, keep the commandments." Would not every right hearted Israelite have understood the whole, but wishing perhaps for ostentation, he saith unto him, Which? Jesus said, Thou shalt do no murder, Thou shalt not commit adultery, Thou shalt not steal, Thou shalt not bear false witness, Honour thy father and thy mother; and thou shalt love

G

thy neighbor as thyself." Here we have only
five enumerated. But does that prove that the
first table, containing the rules of our duty to God,
are all abolished. Certainly that would be bold
deduction, far, rather than fair inference. If
moreover, because the first table of the law is not
here formally expressed, the conclusion must be,
that the four commandments of it are repealed;
why should not the tenth upon the same account
be considered as no more? The Apostle, however, it appears, found the tenth not rescinded, but
still in the list. This he did too, when he was
studying the law, not in the superficial and superstitious way of a Pharisee, but when he was spit-
itually and deeply exercised in religion. He obtained from the law, by the assistance and gracious
operation of the spirit of God, the knowledge of
sin. "I had not known lust, unless the law had
said, Thou shalt not covet." Paul certainly did
not know that all the commandments not mentioned in the foregoing list were abrogated. If
he had, he would not have troubled his conscience
about covetousness, for it appears that his mind,
with all the moral and religious culture which it
had received, could not, or did not, without the
law, discern, or count much upon, heart sins.

It is equally evident and certain, that this relation of his own experience was designed for general edification; of course, he did not allow us to
take the former enumeration of the commandments as entire and complete. But we need not
have left the passage itself to shew that the tenth,

and the four of the first table, containing most formally our duty to God are not excluded. He
mentions a few of the commandments, in order to
direct him to the moral code for the rule of his
obedience. There is great wisdom manifested
however in the selection. They are commandments which respect overt conduct ; as if he had
said, " Live peaceably, chastely, honestly, truly,
dutifully." But does he say this is a perfect
summary of moral and religious duties ? It had
been strange, if he had so mutilated his own law
and neglected altogether the fear of God, which
old testament teachers of eminent rank, by the
spirit of God, pronounce to be the beginning of
wisdom.

Solomon, when in old age and having made
many observations on religious and moral, as well
as on natural things, says, " Fear God and keep
his commandments, for this is the whole duty of
man." Does the Saviour then relax this law, and
say that a man who observed only a part of it
would be perfect ? No. " If thou wilt be perfect, sell what thou hast and give to the poor."
Lo ! Now his conscience feels the painful twitch-
es of the tenth commandment. He had great
possessions. Although the Lord of al , who for
our sakes became poor that we through his pov-
erty might be rich, gave commandment and example, he could not obey. " He went away sor-
rowing." For what was he sorry ?—that he
found the divine teacher, whom he had already
called "Good Master," so strict a casuist, that he

enforced, as he thought, with such severity, the
duties of the moral law. He had perhaps never
before thought of the rights of the poor any farther than the caprice of the rich will grant. His
goods were now by the Lord of all transferred to
the poor. He coveted, notwithstanding, and
kept them. " How hardly shall a rich man enter
into the kingdom of heaven? How hardly shall
they who trust in uncertain riches be saved?
Men must be content in any state which the Lord
of all is pleased to order them, and with another
frame of mind they cannot be his disciples. It
seems then we may add one, viz the tenth to the
previous enumeration and so we shall have at
least six.

But what is to be done with the four of the first
table? Are they all irretrievably gone by the o-
mission of them in this colloquy? No; they are
all included in the command, "take up the cross
and follow me." To follow Jesus no doubt implies that we should avouch him to be our God by
faith in his name, " Ye believe in God, believe
also in me." This he commands to all his followers. By this faith in the Son, all believers
obtain possession of the Father. They receive
the true God as their own and only God. " He
that hath the Son hath the Father."—Though
two persons they are but one God. " I and my
Father are *one.*" " There are three that bear
record in heaven, the Father, the Word and the
Holy Ghost, and these three are one." He was
then evidently commanded in order to be perfect

according to the law, to have the true God for his God. He must renounce his god of gold—he must have the right object of worship, the only true God—he must also worship and glorify him accordingly. This is the first commandment— "Thou shalt have no other Gods before me." He must also be correct in the means of worship, for as there is but one God, so there is but one Mediator between God and man, the man Christ Jesus. There is no image allowable in worship; there is but one that can exhibit the Father, viz. the Son. He and not the gilded statue, or in a diated painting, is the brightness of the Father's glory, and the express image of his person. He is God manifested in the flesh. "No man hath seen God at any time, the only begotten, who is in the bosom of the Father, he hath declared him." They, then, who will follow this, God manifested in the flesh, or in the person of the Son incarnate, must not conform to fashionable and safe modes of worship, as some Judaizers did who had their proselytes circumcised, and so being accounted Jews, the offence of the cross ceased. While the Jews worshipped the true God correctly, the Romans persecuted them. When they rejected the holy One of Israel, the just Jesus, their persecuting cruelty was turned upon the Christians. This man is therefore evidently commanded by the great teacher to take up divine institutions at all peril. He must receive, observe, keep pure and entire all such religious worship and ordinances as God hath ap-

pointed in his word. He must worship exclusively by means of the spirit and essence of divine
appointment. This is the second commandment.
Nor can any follow Jesus and fail to learn obedience to the third precept of the decalogue. The
name of God indeed is put upon the Mediator,
and we never reverence the name of God aright,
until we believe in the name of him whom he hath
sent. His name is a strong tower, to which the
righteous run and are safe. So long as we stand
aloof from the fortress, we defy the prowess and
shew despite to the puissant majesty of the Lord
of hosts. In believing and following Jesus, we
respect the word of God, which he has exalted
above all his name. •We humbly and reverent-
ly take shelter in the promises of the rock of
our salvation. We also respect all those ordinances whereby he makes himself known, rever-
ently use sacraments and prayer, for the honor of
his majesty, as well as our own edification. In
all, therefore, which respects the mode of worship,
or the principle of the third commandment, the
followers of Jesus will learn reverence. Christ
taught his disciples to say in confidence, " Our
Father."—He also taught them that he was not a
Father on earth, but a Father in heaven. Through
him, as the great high priest, we may draw near,
in the full assurance of faith; but we must also
have our hearts sprinkled from an evil conscience
and our bodies washed in pure water. " Having
a kingdom which cannot be moved, we must have
grace, whereby we may serve God acceptably in

reverence and godly fear. For *our* God is a con--
suming fire. If therefore we do not fear and rev--
erence the great and dreadful name of the Lord
our God, he will make our plagues wonderful.

It will be then only the fourth commandment
that can be any way doubtful, and even that we
expect to shew is yet obligatory on the followers,
of Jesus. It is not doubted that there are some
naughty children who would rather have a play
day, than a holy day. It may be also that there
are some, who say they have experienced religion,
and so have made a profession, who yet would
reckon the strict sanctification of the sabbath a
weariness. Such will very readily argue that
Christ has relieved us from all the burdens of a
legal dispensation.

Sure however I am, that no fair candidate for
the rest which remains for the people of God, no
good apprentice for the employment of heaven,
would reckon himself more free, if he had no day
in seven exclusively allowed and appointed for
religious duties and holy exercises. The best, it
is true, fail in this duty of sabbath sanctification
as in all others. "*When* I would do good," says
Paul, "evil is present with me." What more?
Is it, O wretched law, who shall deliver me from
thy burdensome precepts! No—"But O wretched man, who shall deliver me from the body of
this death? I thank God through Jesus Christ.
So then, with the *mind* I myself serve the law of
God." This he would not say if he had a heart
hatred of the fourth commandment. The fourth

commandment not only occupies a central place
in the body, but also in the spirit of the law or ten
commandments. It is prefaced in such a manner
as to shew, in concurrence with the ancient history of its institution, that it was of a date long
prior to the legation of Moses. The word "Remember" however shews how ready we are to
forget it, and how permanently important it is,
that we should hold it in constant remembrance.

Men of the most noted science, in law and religion, have decided, from experience and observation in favor of what this preface implies.
Judge Hale remarked that even in his worldly
concerns he always found it disadvantigeous not
to remember, with great strictness, the Sabbath-
day. What was still more evincible of his christian spirit, he wished that it might always be so.
Thousands of observing christians have no doubt
observed the same thing, in the dispensations of
Providence towards themselves and others.
Where is there a neighborhood that cannot relate
numerous anecdotes of divine judgment evidently
executed upon the violation of the laws of the
Sabbath? Is it likely then that Providence would
so uniformly sanction the observation of a law
which is abrogated? The arrangements of the
system of nature clearly point out the propriety of
observing about a seventh part of our time. The
phases of the moon vary about every seventh day.
This indication like all the intimations of nature,
is to be sure comparatively dark. What then?
Why evidently, that we should attend to the clear
light of supernatural revelation.

If heathen nations count time by months and weeks, and of their weeks keep particularly one day holy, should not we who have better instruction and greater encouragement ? Almost all Christian societies observe one day in seven, or profess to do so. Have they divine authority for this or is it will worship ? They do it. Is not this an acknowledgement that this commandment is salutary ? Can we then suppose that the Saviour came to abolish a *salutary* statute ?—That the Redeemer, who came to deliver us from the bondage of sin and secular care, would abrogate a precept so eminently desirable and useful for that express purpose ? Is it likely that he, who not only taught men himself, but also appointed a permanent order of men to communicate publicly religious instruction to others would leave them for this purpose no time ? Would the God of order leave it to every one's option when that sanctified precious time should be ? Would it not produce confusion and destroy sabbatic order and the order of society, if one should keep the first, another the fourth, and a third the last day of the week ? Is it probable that he who came to give direction and instruction to his ransomed children concerning the kingdom of heaven, that he would leave it so, that of this rest they would have no pledge, no earnest, that they would have no stated *time* to prepare for *eternity* ? There may be *some*, who, for purposes of their own, may think all these things probable ; there cannot be many such who, *think* at all upon them. But still it will be objected,

First, That the fourth commandment appoints the seventh day. Second, That the observation of a seventh part of time is not moral in its nature, nor particularly commanded in the New Testament. Third, That in the New Testament dispensation all times and places are alike, i. e. there is no time or place holy.

To the first we reply; that the fourth commandment does contain a circumstantial allusion to the original reason of keeping the seventh day. "For in six days the Lord made heaven and earth, the sea, and all that in them is, and rested the seventh day." But it must also be observed that in the solemn formal appointment, and special consecration and benediction, he only mentions the seventh part of time as the sabbath day. It is not, 'Remember the seventh day'; but "remember the *sabbath day* to keep it holy, i. e. Remember to observe such set times as God appoints in his word for holy rest. Six days shalt thou labour and do all thy work, but the seventh day is the Sabbath. This is just as much and as punctually observed by the industrious and pious christian who labors six days to provide for himself and his own household, and who rests one, viz. the first, to attend with his family on private and public acts of religion, as it was by the obedient Jew. In rendering the reason too of this observance it is not said, " God blessed the seventh day and hallowed or consecrated it, but " God blessed the *sabbath day*," &c. not saying particularly what day it should be. Was this chance, or was it design? If it was chance it was evidently an ill chance, for those who plead either for the seventh day sabbath, or for the abolition of the fourth commandment.

Whatever the superstitious and censorious Pharisee might think of the disciples, because they plucked the ears of corn, and refreshed their hungry and fatigued bodies, as they were going to meeting, it is evident from our Saviour's allowing and vindicating it, that works of obvious necessity, mercy and piety, were not forbidden upon this day.

It is equally evident that the command to labor six days, was only in order that all their secular, ordinary and servile labor might be done upon these, because while the commandment was, by all considered obligatory, there were many days appointed for religious and ceremonial services.

These facts then shew that the fourth commandment in sanctioning the observation of the first day Sabbath, does not hinder or forbid the occasional observation of other days in religious services, nor yet the performance of necessary and merciful works on the Lord's day. If it did either, then it was inconsistent with the by laws of Old Testament times, as well as with ecclesiastical enactments, & Christian usage in the New.

The Old Testament writers by prophetic vision saw the change of the order of the days. In perfect consistency with their fullest belief of the *permanent sanction of the Moral Law,* and the standing authority of the fourth commandment they wrote of the change from the seventh to the first day. Beyond all question, when speaking prophetically of our times, they contemplate the continuance of Sabbatic institutions. Without this indeed they would have considered the dispensation inferior to their own, and would not have wished to see such a time. Thus the prophet and psalmist David, in the cxviii Psalm, after having sung the sufferings of Christ, he sings also his following glory :—"The stone which the builders rejected the same is become the head of the corner." When did this take place? The gospel will tell you that it was the day in which he rose from the dead, or first day of the week. He was there ; he was declared to be the Son of God with power, by his resurrection from the dead.

But the same eminent type of our Lord, in allusion to the same time, says, " This is the day which the Lord hath made ; we will rejoice and be glad in it." It is evident that this day must be considered as some how peculiarly made. He has made all the days, in a certain sense, for he teaches the planets to revolve, whereby day and night, and seasons of the year are measured. All these vicissitudes are regulated by the great Jehovah. What then is particular upon this day mentioned by the prophet David? Every christian can readily answer this. It was on *this day his* Son, " the sun of righteousness arose." He will therefore be particularly glad in it. This

is the day. God hath made evangelical light to
shine out of great darkness, and so should be a
day in which hosannas should be sung, and salvation declared in Sion. On this day should the
souls and the bodies of the redeemed be affectionately bound to the altar of instituted worship,
that they may be offered living sacrifices, holy
and acceptable to God. On this day, Christians
will rejoice to receive blessings from the Church
or house of the Lord. In holy elation of mind
they will give thanks to God in remembrance of
his grace and mercy, which continues forever in
the appointment and continuance of means and
times of administering salvation.

Such is the view which the psalmist took of our
privileged times. Alas! that so many who enjoy the advantages of these times should pro-
fessionally or practically obscure their glory.
Isaiah, the evangelical prophet, who like David
speaks of the sufferings and glory of Christ, rather in the language of history than of prophecy,
saw the continued observation of the Sabbath as
a Christian duty and a Christian privilege. In
the fifty-sixth chapter, where he prophecies of
the accession of all people to the Church or house
of the Lord, he says in the name of the Lord,
"keep ye judgment, and do justice, for my salvation is near to come, and my righteousness to be
revealed. Blessed is the man that doeth this,
and the son of man that layeth hold on it, that
keepeth the sabbath from polluting it, and keepeth his hand from any evil." The poor eunuch
H

was not only a dry tree in the state, but also was excluded from dwelling in the temple, performing its service, or enjoying its privilege. But not so in the dispensation of which he prophecies. He and the Gentile stranger are to have their place in this more liberal dispensation of the covenant of grace. Still however they are not to neglect the Sabbath. This would be the lazy, licentious liberty of the profligate reprobate, not the glorious liberty of the sons and children of God. " For thus saith the Lord unto the eunuchs that keep my sabbaths and choose the things that please me, and take hold of my covenant ; even unto them will I give in mine house and within my walls, a name better than of sons and of daughters : I will give them an everlasting name that shall not be cut off. Also the sons of the stranger that join themselves unto the Lord to serve him, and to love the name of the Lord, to be his servants every one that *keepeth the Sabbath* from polluting it, and taketh hold of my covenant, even them will I bring to my holy mountain and make them joyful in my house of prayer. These sacrifices shall be acceptable, for my house shall be called a house of prayer for *all people*."

Can any thing be more obvious than that the prophet had a gospel scene before him, and yet he saw a sabbath ? It is true he beheld sacrifices also ; but have we no sacrifices ? Yes, certainly. The sacrifices of a broken and contrite heart—of doing good and communicating—of offering our souls and bodies were always pleasing sacrifices in his sight, and still are a reasonable service. The time then of which the prophet speaks, must synchronise with the time of which Christ says— "Neither in mount Gerizim nor yet in Jerusalem shall men worship the Father, that is exclusively, but every where men shall call on the Lord, and be accepted." And when did this take place? After the advent of Messiah, or in New Testament times: and yet according to the prophet, there is a sabbath to be kept from polluting it. Ezekiel also, xlii. chapter, 27th verse prophesies of the same time and of the change and observation of the sabbath day. "And it shall be, when those days are expired, that upon the eighth day and so forward, the priest shall make your burnt offerings upon the altar, and your peace offerings, and I will accept you, saith the Lord God."

Our Christian sabbath is upon the eighth day from creation, and so forward. Upon that day spiritual sacrifices are accepted. By this change, if you just consider that mournful day in which the disciples had no rest, because they thought their Master was gone, never more to return, blotted out of the calendar of christians, the first day sabbath just comes in its room—a day in which their troubled minds were comforted and restored to rest, in the manifestations of their risen Redeemer. At any rate, it is very evident, count as you will, that the fourth commandment was always practicable. There never was a week without a sabbath; there never was a week with two. Although the day was changed from the seventh to the first, or as the Prophet expresses it, "on the eighth day, and so forward, the priests shall offer your burnt offerings, &c. and I will accept you still it was the sabbath of the Lord God, as we will more fully shew.

Second objection. That the observance of a seventh part of time is not a duty of nature, and not particularly commanded in the New Testament.

Answer. We have already proved with relation to the tenth commandment, that it is not necessary that a law, which shall be accounted moral and permanent, shou'd be obvious to our natural understanding and unrenewed conscience. It is enough that the observance of it be found permanently to be of practical utility. We are not to conclude neither that nothing is discoverable which we have not discovered. Nature teaches us as a theorem, that there is a God, and as a problem or practical maxim, that he is to be worshipped. I cannot see why it is not as evident, that he is to be worshipped on some fixed or appointed time, as that he should be worshipped at all. We may not be able perhaps to shew by the light of nature, that the seventh part is more proper than the sixth or eighth part. I presume, notwithstanding, that none but cavillers will say, that there is therefore no more propriety in the one arrangement than there would be in the other.

It is clear, that in all ages, social man has observed the seventh part of time, and counted days by weeks. It is from this circumstance that we have the epithet Sunday, as the name of the first day of the week. None can be at any loss to know from whence it received that name. On the first day light was made. Although this light was not regularly organized or incorporated into the body of the sun, or into distinct and various luminous bodies, as it afterwards was on the fourth day; yet it is evident, that it was so conglomerated and the revolutions of the earth so ordered, that there was evening and morning or alternate darkness and light. That day then, on which it was first seen to rise, not from a previous circuit on another hemisphere, but from the hand of the Father of lights, has very naturally been called Sunday.

We do not plead for the propriety of that unscriptural and heathen name of the Lord's day or Christian sabbath. Some of the Fathers, who wished to be understood by Grecian and Roman readers, gave it that title. But it certainly is worthy of remark, that the Sun of Righteousness, the Sun of the world of grace, rose upon the same day as did the sun of nature. In both cases, it is evident the darkness must have been before the light. The evening or dark time, and the morning or light time, was the first day. It is clear on the least reflection that the first day did not, could not, begin nor end with sunset; and it is equally evident, that the first day, upon which Christ rose, did not begin with sun-set, nor end. Very early in the morning, while it was yet dark, the women

came to the sepulchre : In the evening of the
same day, when the disciples were assembled and
the doors shut, Christ met with them. John xx·
1, 19. · Whatever therefore·may be the practice
of the Jews, and some congregational churches,·
who begin the Sabbath from sun-set of Saturday,
and end it at sun-set of Sabbath, it does not appear that from the beginning either of the world
of nature, or of the world of grace that it was so.
The practice of the reforming ruler Nehemiah
has been quoted as authority for this practice.
I do not see, however, what end it answers to
those who cite it: It seems indeed rather against
them.   He first testified against the profane merchants of Judah themselves, who brought their
wares into market on that day.   Reproof he knew
would be cast away upon the Tyrian hucksters
who brought fish into Jerusalem.   He reproved
the police nobles, however, because they tolerated
such trade on the Sabbath. · In the third place he
ordered the gate to be shut.   When? Why when
it began to be dark *before the Sabbath*, and in the
fourth place, when they would yet profane the
sabbath by lying about the walls, to be in early
after the sabbath was over, he threatened, if they
persisted in this, that he would lay hands on them.
This is a true statement of the matter, and what
is there in it that favours the beginning and end-
ing of the Sabbath with sun-set ?   That you may
have it before you in studying the matter, recite
the passage as it stands. Neh. xiii. 15. "In those
days I saw in Judah some treading wine presses

on the sabbath, and bringing in sheaves, and lading asses : as also wine, grapes and figs, and all manner of burdens, which they brought into Jerusalem on the sabbath day ; and I testified against them in the day wherein they sold victuals. There dwelt men of Tyre also therein, which brought fish, and all manner of ware, and sold on the sabbath unto the children of Judah and in Jerusa'em. Then I contended with the nobles of Judah, and said unto them, What evil thing is this that ye do, and profane the sabbath day ? Did not your fathers thus, and did not your God bring all this evil upon us, and upon this city ? yet ye bring more wrath upon Israel by profaning the sabbath. And it came to pass that when the gates of Jerusalem began to be dark before the Sabbath, I commanded that the gates should be shut, and charged that they shou'd not be opened till after the sabbath : and some of my servants 'set I at the gates, that there should be no burden brought in on the sabbath day. So the merchants and sellers of all kinds of ware lodged without Jerusalem once or twice. Then I testified against them, and said unto them, Why lodge ye about the wall ? if ye do so again I will lay hands on you. From that time forth came they no more on the sabbath."

We readily grant that this conduct was influenced by the spirit of true religion, and left upon record with divine approbation, to be a copy for imitation to all Christian magistrates that would study the welfare of the people, over whom they

rule; but how it proves the propriety of com-
mencing and terminating the sabbath with the going down of the sun, I have yet to learn. Indeed
this way appears to me contrary to the nature of
things and contrary to the nature of man. According to this plan, there would be no sabbath in
some parts, for a considerable time. Again,
weeks yea, months, all sabbath. In polar regions,
the sun is about six months above, and about six
months below the horizon. How are these people to measure their weeks? Are they to make
their weeks weeks of years, and their sabbath,
when it occurs, from equinox to equinox? Ab-
rupt transitions, shou'd men all live in low lati-
tudes, are very inconvenient. Sometimes in fog-
gy weather too, we do not exactly know when
the sun sets.

The sabbath ought, and does begin and terminate in the still hour of midnight.

There is no necessity of being scrupulous about
the same absolute time, in which others may be
engaged in worship and sabbath keeping. To
this mode of calculating there would be no end of
distinction. However proper it may be to shut
gates and put a stop to the hurry of business on
the evening before the sabbath, this does not begin the sabbath, but is preparatory for it. Even
should it be proved, that the Jewish sabbath did
begin with sun-set, that will not prove that our's
ought, any more than it will prove, that our sabbath should be the seventh day of the week, as
their's was. We can easily see how Christ was

part of three days in the grave, whether we begin the day with sun-set or midnight. The way, it appears, that the Jews computed time, was this: They counted the night by watches or periods of three hours each, and the day by hours. The first watch of the night was from sun-set or six o'clock to nine—the second watch from nine to twelve, or midnight—the third, from twelve to three in the morning—the fourth, or morning watch from three to six. Their day again was computed from six or sun-rise. From the sixth to the seventh, according to the Roman computation, or as we would say, from six to seven, they called the first hour of the day—from seven to eight, the second, from eight to nine the third, &c. It appears too that about such an hour signifies, in their style, when that hour had nearly expired. Thus about the sixth hour seems to intimate that it was about noon, at which time the sixth hour of their day transpired. At the third hour or nine o'clock A. M. Christ was nailed upon the cross. Mark xv. 25. About the sixth hour or noon, the darkness commenced, and continued till the ninth hour or three P. M. Math. xxvii. 45. Luke xxiii. 44. About this time nature was all convulsed—the vail rent—the graves opened—the earth quaked. The centurion confessed—"He glorified God, saying, Certainly this was a righteous man. And all the people that came together to that sight, beholding the things which were done, smote their breasts and returned." All seemed to have been moved with hor-

ror of sympathy but the rotten hearted pharisees.
They were insensible to all feeling, but that of
envy and hate. They pretended however to zeal
and strictness. John xix. 31. The Jews therefore
because it was the preparation; that the bodies
should not remain upon the cross on the sabbath
day, (for that sabbath was an high day) besought
Pilate that their legs might be broken, &c.

The Ecclesiastics of that time would never
have effected the nefarious deeds they did, had
they not affected great piety. The dead bodies
must therefore be interred before the sabbath.
The necessity of fracturing the limbs, however,
of the Saviour, was superceded by his previous
decease. His agony of mind in bearing our sins,
his scourging by Pilate, and perhaps his voluntary surrender of his soul to the Father, when his
work was finished, rendered this act unnecessary.
The executioners when they came to him found
his body dead; they pierced his heart with a
spear, but broke not his bones that the scripture
might be fulfilled, "A bone of him shall not be
broken." Joseph of Arimathea and Nicodemus,
both men of eminence in the Church and Commonwealth of Israel, bestowed pains and cost upon his funeral. While alive, they were under
strong convictions that he was the Messiah of
promise, but they did not publicly confess him.
Now when his own disciples fled, forsook and
denied him, they acknowledge him—Joseph gives
him his new tomb. Nicodemus brings a copious
and costly preparation of spices and aromatic

drugs to perfume his lacerated body—they wrap it in linen clothes with the spices, as the Jews' custom is to bury. By this time it must have been about evening. Still, however, it is the preparation, and the sabbath only drew on. Luke xxiii. 54. The women visited the sepulchre, returned, prepared spices also before it was necessary to rest on the sabbath, according to the scriptures. Had they considered the sabbath over too at sun-set, why should they not have visited the tomb that evening rather than early on the first day of the week, while it was yet dark? But admitting the Jews did count their days, as Persians and some Eastern nations do, Christ was laid in the tomb on the afternoon of the sixth day. That, according to Jewish computation, is counted one. He continues in the tomb all the seventh, that is two, a part of the first, that is the third day, in which he rose. But if you begin the first day from sunset, you cannot possibly make out a part of three days in which he continued in the grave. However then the fact be about the Jewish sabbath, the christian sabbath cannot, with any propriety, begin earlier than midnight, nor can it end earlier, unless you would say that it began before the Saviour rose, and you might as well begin the era of his birth before he was born, or the commemoration of his resurrection before he rose. Of this again, in relation to the second part of the exception, we would remark, that we have no express commandment in the New Testament to keep this or any other day as a sabbath. The commandment we have seen was not repealed. All that was necessary was that we should see an example whereby we would know what day it was that the commandment now respected. This we have clearly set before us, in the example of the Apostles, who, during the forty days of our Saviour's abode upon earth, *after* the resurrection, had an opportunity to receive directions concerning the affairs of the Church or kingdom of heaven. It is clear that their first interview with him after his death, was upon this memorable day. Again, it is said, eight days after. There certainly may be something learned from this chronological relation: It was written, no doubt, for this purpose. The second Lord's day they were all met. Although Thomas had his unbelieving doubts, yet he met that day and had his doubts removed. Upon this first day also the Holy Spirit, with which they were to be endowed for their great work, descended. The passover that year we have already seen happened upon a Jewish sabbath. Seven of these will bring us to the forty-ninth day, for they counted from the passover. Their Pentecost or feast which happened on the fiftieth day after the passover, would, of course, be upon a first day of the week. On the day of Pentecost however you know the Spirit descended; therefore it is evident he descended upon the first day of the week or Lord's day. The disciples were there assembled upon that day.

Seven weeks had now transpired since his resurrection. On the first day, the same in which

he arose, a little better than a week after our
Lord's ascension the Promised Comforter vouch-
safed his presence, his remarkable presence
among the disciples and assembled Jews. We
shall see afterwards, that the Spirit from on high
did not teach them nor us to desist from the
sanctification of the first day of the week as the
Christian sabbath. Nay, if He had not designed
to countenance it, He would not have appeared
on that day, for it is evident, they were already
habituated to the practice. The Apostles were
influenced in a very immediate manner by their
divine Teacher in planting the Churches, and is
it not most clear, that they were in the habit of
keeping the first day of the week as a Sabbath?
It can easily be made to appear that the Apostolic Churches were wont to assemble on that day
for religious worship, such as prayer, praise,
charitable contributions and communion. Acts
xx. 7th, 1 Cor. xvi. 1, may, with many other passages of scripture, be adduced as proof. There
is one thing to be observed from the first of these
places just now cited, that I do not remember of
ever seeing noticed, viz. that although the Apostle continued his speech till midnight, he seems
to have considered it still the first day of the
week. "And upon the first day of the week,
when the disciples came together to break bread,
Paul preached unto them, and continued his
speech until midnight." It appears, that these ancient primitive christians and their preacher had
not yet learned, that the sabbath or first day of the

I

week, ended till that time. Luke too, the writer of the book, considered that the second day had not yet commenced, for he states that Paul was ready to depart on the morrow.

It cannot be admitted that the precept in 1 Cor. xvi. 1, was either local or temporary. In the very face of it, it bears the evident mark of a catholic and abiding commandment. I am sorry, however, that with a part of it, the societies under my charge do not comply. " Now concerning the collection for the saints, as I have given commandment to the churches of Galatia, even so do ye. Upon the first day of the week, let every one of you lay by him in store as God hath prospered him." From this canon, it is evident that the Apostle calculated, that whatever occasional meetings the Churches might have, that they would have constant and stated meetings on the first day, or Christian sabbath—that their thanksgiving services on the Lord's day should have something practical—that they should make a collection and so raise a fund for charitable and religious purposes. The saints at Jerusalem had a very primary and particular claim upon the Churches' charity. Many in that place had sold their possessions and goods, and laid them at the feet of the Apostles. By this means the wants of the indigent exiles abroad had been supplied, and missionaries had been supported in conveying good news to distant regions, before the Churches were so organized as to make provision for the support of the gospel ministers. The

saints in Jerusalem, by the terrible calamities
which preceded the entire destruction of that me-
tropolis, had been reduced to want and indigence
themselves. On principles, therefore, of recipro-
city, as well as on principles of charity, other
Churches, less affected by these revolutionary
tribulations, felt themselves bound to make contribution to their necessities and reimbursements
of their former kindness. The first day of the
week, was the day on which this deed of charity
was to be done. And so long as there are poor
with us, it would be well to observe this injunction.

It was an ancient practice among the Jews, and
had divine sanction, that none was to come before
God with his hands empty. Our Saviour approves of the woman's contribution of her last
mite into the Lord's treasury. He assures us
that we have the poor always with us. It is sanctioned by the almost universal practice of all
christians; it is congruous with the principles of
our nature, that when the charities of our hearts
are enlivened by the doctrines and spirit of true
religion, our hands should be opened to acts of
charity and religious bounty.

As to the *third objection,* we just say that it
does not very well comport with the practice of
Congregational and Baptist Churches, who con-
secrate or dedicate their meeting-houses.

I do not know, however, that place or time
could ever be said to be holy in themselves only
on account of the services to be performed in

them, or on account of what they symbolised. The
temple and its furniture were holy, as types of
Christ. He is come to the great antitypical temple. Destroy, says he, pointing to his body, this
temple, and I will rear it up in three days, speaking of the temple of his body. To that personal
temple we must still look in presenting our services, wherever we reside, by the banks of the
Chebar or of the Connecticut. He will hear in
heaven, who dwells bodily in Immanuel. Now
there is no need, of course, that Jews and Samar-
itans should dispute about hills, such as Gerizim
and Sion, or Jews and Christians about new moon
Sabbaths, or Papists and Protestants about
Christmas and other holy days, as those call the
days they have dedicated to saints. But it would
require more than the *ipse dixit* of disputants to
prove, that one day in seven according to the last
of the fourth commandment, is not as holy as it
ever was. If it is not, what have we in its room?
We have seen what we have in lieu of the consecrated temple. What have we in lieu of the sabbath? Christ says plainly, that there should be a
sabbath after the establishment of Christianity or
of the new Testament administration. Math.
xxiv. 20. "But pray ye that your flight be not in
the winter, or on *the Sabbath day*." He is here
speaking of the flight of Christians from the
smoking ruins of Jerusalem. The destruction of
this once famous city took place many years after
the ascension of our Lord. Let the objector
then tell what the object was, that would be gain-

ed by the answer of this prayer. His argument admits that the Jewish sabbath was no more.

What legal or moral impediments then would be in the way of flight? The Jewish laws could not be operative in Palestine, when Jerusalem was about to be devoured by Romish torches. The Romans would not hinder them to fly upon that day. There might be natural obstacles and difficulties peculiar in the winter. But if there was no holy time, or Christian sabbath, what was the moral difficulty to be averted by this prayer, that their flight might not be on the sabbath day. Every intelligent Christian sees the object at once. He knows that flight from an enemy is a work of necessity, but he is piously solicitous that such necessity might not be imposed. All such therefore would devoutly pray, that they might not be forced to forego the privileges of one day of holy rest, because every true christian highly prizes this time and reckons, with the man after God's own heart, a day in God's courts better than a thousand; he reckons all things loss for the excellency of the knowledge of Christ. He wishes to enjoy repose from worldly fears as well as cares, that he may muse upon the mysteries and achievements of the Redeemer, the Lord of that day; he wishes to wait without distraction upon the administration of the gospel, which he knows God is pleased to make the power of God and the wisdom of God unto salvation. He therefore prays that his flight be not on the Christian sabbath day.

I 2

The Apostle reasons strongly in proof of the continuance of a sabbath for Christians. Heb. iv. 9. " There remaineth yet a rest (or as it is in the original, a sabbatism or keeping of a sabbath) for the people of God," 'for' says he, "He that hath entered into his rest, h. th ceased from his works as God did from his." How was that? How did God cease from his works? This is well known to all who are acquainted with the sacred history of the origin of things. God ceased from his works of creation on the seventh day, and hallowed it for a Sabbath, a holy rest. If then the Son, who laboured in the work of redemption during the toilsome week of his sublunary travel, has imitated this example of God the Father, he has also consecrated the first day of the week, as a christian Sabbath of holy and spiritual rest for all the inhabitants of the new world, and subjects of the new creation of the Holy Spirit. The Apostle had before proved, that the antitype of the seventh day rest, or Jewish sabbath, was not the land of Canaan into which Jesus or Joshua, which is the same name, only the former Greek, the latter Hebrew, had introduced them. He proves this from what David, so long after this introduction said. In the xcv. psalm, David, speaking in the name and by the Spirit of his Master, says v. 10. "Forty years long was I grieved with this generation, and said it is a people that do err in their heart, and they have not known my ways: v. 11. Unto whom I swear in, my wrath that they should not enter into my rest."

The Apostle quotes from the Septuagint, and says "If they shall enter into my rest," i. e. such characters shall not.

We readily admit, that this may refer to the privileges of a gospel state, as Dr. Owen understands it, and to the eternal rest of heaven, as Baxter and others explain it. But neither the profound Owen, nor the fervent Baxter, nor their explanations would oppose this inference. Nay, the fact that it does respect these things is in favour of our argument and against the objector. Is the gospel state a Sabbatism, and yet the fourth commandment in its spirit, as well as form, repealed? No sabbath day among Christians travelling to the Canaan of heavenly rest!!!

Finally, in answer to this objection, hear what John calls the Christian sabbath. Rev. 1, 10. " I was in the spirit on the Lord's day." Does not this clearly express the peculiar holiness of this time? If not, why called his? Is not the Lord's supper a holy supper?—the Lord's table a holy table?—the Lord's people a holy people? Why then should not the Lord's day be counted really, properly, and exclusively a HOLY DAY?

From these details of argument then, it must appear, that the moral law continues in all its *integrity*, in all its *utility*, and in all its *sanction*.

The very circumstance that Christ did not give a new law, will be to the judicious and candid pretty strong evidence, that I e did not destroy the integrity of the old. That the law did exist, when he came in the flesh, was a fact too well known to be overlooked ;—too practically important to be neglected and no improvement be made of it. If then something must be done with the law by the great Legislator when upon earth, we cannot conceive of his disposing of that law otherwise than one of these three ways. He must either, First—Disannul it altogether and totally, or, Second—Abrogate a part, and ratify a part, or, Third—Ratify and sanction the whole. Had he intended to do the first, he must have proceeded in the business of abrogation in a style which could not be misunderstood. The Truth could not equivocate about, or deny any object of his mission. It is true, in some, instances he eluded the snares of his adversaries, who thought to entangle him in his speech. The Pharisees and Herodians differed in their views of politics. The former were professedly zealous for the ancient rights of the Israelitish constitution and divine charter. The latter were temporizers and professed to admire the administration of Herod. They thought to improve this dispute by prefering a case to Christ, which would force him either to speak what the Pharisees would make treason against God, or the Herodians against Cæsar. They ask therefore--Is it lawful to give tribute to Cæsar or not? He eluded this ensnaring question, about which he knew they had their minds already made up, by saying, Render unto Cæsar the things which are Caesar's, and to God the things which are God's.

On another time they thought to make him

speak what they would construe blasphemy, "By
what authority dost thou these things, and who
gave thee this authority? He asks them about
the baptism of John, whether it was from heaven
or from men. They found themselves perplex-
ed and embarrassed. If they said from heaven,
they knew he would say, Why hear ye not him?
If they said of men, they feared the people, for
they all held John as a prophet: They therefore
say, We cannot tell. He says, Neither tell I
you by what authority I do these things. In
such cases as these it is clear that instruction was
neither candidly sought, nor professedly given:
But did he ever conceal his design from his disciples, or speak obscurely to his followers about
what he came to teach? Or did he ever hint to
them that he came to destroy the law? Had he
done so it must have been accounted for. His
disciples were not the licentious rabble that false
teachers usually pick up, and easily proselyte to
any loose system. They were sober men, taught
in the religion of their times, and especially
taught and accustomed to revere the law. If
then the law was to be abrogated, there must be
a full and satisfactory discussion of this matter.
Where is this discussion to be found? Rather,
where is the contrary not to be found?

If any such thing could be found, it certainly
would have been easy in that state of society to
have condemned him, without suborning false and
inconstant witnesses in order to establish a libel
against Jesus. If nothing such can be found, is

it not strange that such an improbable thing can
be, now surmised against Christ? It cannot be
said that he designed to lay aside the law; but
suppressed his design for fear of popular rage.
Than this suggestion there can be nothing more
absurd and horrid. It is absurd and contradictory. It says he did, and did not lay it aside.
How is his design to this effect known, seeing
through fear and policy he suppressed it? But
how could he be influenced by either of these base
passions? His professed design was to die—he
came to lay down his life a ransom for many.
What then could one that had death as a part of
his plan fear? He sought not, nay he refused,
promotion from the people. "I receive not honour from men." "My kingdom is not of this
world." He raised no bustle of ambitious striving for mastery in the streets of civil polity—he
only came to bear witness for the truth and suffer for his people's salvation who had violated
the law. In doing so it was necessary he should
fu'fil all righteousness.

Did this look like abrogating the whole law?
We sometimes learn the nature of a teacher's
doctrine from the conduct of his scholars. If he
came to disannul the law, we would certainly see
some evidence of it in the conduct of his disciples
and followers. Did they manifest a lawless and
licentious disposition? The very reverse. It
must here be remembered that the law is in every
respect contrary to the corrupt inclinations of
men. Of course, if its restraints were removed

we would immediately see the effects. Do we
see them in the conduct of Christ's followers?
No, but the very contrary. Their conduct is
tried by severe scrutiny in the hands of a censorious world, and still the conduct of Christians,
deficient as they are, is better than that of any
other society of men that ever appeared in the
world. This is not the award and decision of
the Church herself respecting her own members,
but is the opinion of the candid; and an inference
which may be drawn from the judgment of the
malicious. In most cases, among men, more dependance will be put upon the man who is supposed to be influenced by Christian principles,
than upon one destitute of the fear of God.
Why so? if Christ came to lay the law aside, and
the tendency of his doctrine be Antimonian?
The censorious always criticise more rigidly upon the morals of Christians than upon any others.
Why so? Because more is expected from them.
But why is more expected from them? Because
their principles are more strict and their conduct
generally more correct. And does this intimate
that their Master came to destroy the whole
law? Certainly not; but the reverse, that he
came to establish it. These reflections certainly
more than prove that he did not come to repeal
the whole law. Let us next see a little further;
if he came to repeal a part of it.

It must here be remembered that He is speaking of the moral law, summarily comprehended
in the decalogue or ten commandments. If He

had done this, it is clear he must have been explicit in declaring what He ratified and what he repealed. Where then is the place in the history of his transactions, where this is done? There is no such place. It cannot be done by any other. The law is a complete system: you cannot break upon it, without destroying it entirely. He that said, Do not commit adultery, said also, Do not kill. We do not say, with the stoics that all sins are equal—that it is as great a sin to steal a cabbage plant out of a neighbor's garden, as to kill a father. But we do say that every sin is an insult of the majesty and authority of the law; that he who breaks one, or offends in one point, is, in this respect, guilty of all. So far then from there being any evidence, that he has repealed some, there is all evidence against it, and this if possible is more absurd than the former, viz. that he has repealed the whole. There remains therefore no conclusion, but that he has ratified the whole. Whose therefore breaketh one of the least of these commandments, and teacheth men so, shall be called least in the kingdom of heaven. I came not to destroy the law but to fulfil it. Heaven and earth shall pass away, but one iota or tittle of the law shall not pass till all be fulfilled.

In the next place we infer, the *utility* of the law of God. The law of God is useful in showing us what we are; what we ought to be; and what we ought to do. One of the wise sayings of Grecian philosophy was—"*Gnothi seauton*,"

Know thyself. A famous English apothegm is analogous to this. "The proper knowledge of mankind is man." When we examine any person, or any thing we must have some rule by which to conduct the investigation. The law is the rule of personal self-examination, When we examine ourselves by others, we are apt to be proud, and say with the Pharisee, "I thank thee that I am not as other men are." There are two reasons for this. In the first place, were the persons and their characters compared alike; we are partial to ourselves. In the second place, we are partial to those features of character and items of morality, in which we excel. Do we measure ourselves by ourselves, and compare ourselves with ourselves? If we do, we are not wise, Who would not smile at the man who would measure a bushel by itself, to see if it held as much as it held? Would we not think the man deranged who would compare a crooked stick with a crooked stick to see if it was straight? Equally ludicrous and mad is the conduct of the man who makes, from his own mind, the standard of character and morality, and then proceeds to examine himself by this capricious model. We may deceive ourselves when we have the law, but we must deceive ourselves if we proceed in this business without the law. We may deceive ourselves by reckoning that speculative notions are true faith. This is a mistake even should these notions be correct. Fallen spirits may have a correct creed. " Devils believe and tremble."

K

It is very possible to hold the truth in unrighteousness; "For the heart to be without knowledge is not good," says the wisest of men, and
yet, in perfect consistency with this inspired adage
the Apostle intimates that a man may have all
knowledge and yet want charity.

We are liable to self-deception too about feeling and experience. The command is very peremptory and emphatical—"Son, give me thine
heart." The same authority commands—"Rejoice with them that do rejoice, and weep with
them that weep." When we consider our relation to our Creator, Redeemer and Sanctifier,
what can be more reasonable than a compliance
with the former precept? When we consider
our relation to our brethren by natural and religious ties, our mutual dependence and reciprocal
interests, can the propriety of the latter injunction
be doubted? But the difficulty is, we call that a
compliance which is not. How many are there
that think they are loving God and their neigh-
bours, when they are loving themselves? See
that gay lady weeping at the tragic tale related on
the stage; she thinks her heart is tender, and she
prides herself in her sympathetic feelings; but
although she can give a dollar for her ticket to
the box of the theatre, she grudges half a dollar
to the poor box in the Church —She sobs and
cries very affectionately over artificial distress de-
picted by the base actor, but spurns real sorrow
from her door with a bosom cold as Greenland
snow, and a heart hard as the northern steel.

True christians are represented in scripture as sighing and crying for the abominations of the land; they are commanded to pray always. "Blessed are they that mourn, for they shall be comforted." But still, what are we to think of that morose old man, who would never be suspected of christianity but for his long face, long prayers and long relation of experience. If you talk with him about the state of society, his heart is ready to break that the world is so wicked; but what did he ever do to improve it? His notions of religion are narrow and incorrect; the God he worships is as far from being the true God of the scriptures as Baal or Moloch, and yet he thinks himself, and is thought by many, to be a very eminent Christian. His opinion about religion is the oracle of truth to a neighborhood. How useful is the law of God to keep us from such deception! It inculcates active piety—" If ye love me keep my commandments."—" I shall not be ashamed when I have respect to all thy statutes"—' Whatsoever things I have commanded observe and do'—' By the law, then, is the knowledge of sin." This law, however, must not be mutilated in some part, and magnified in others, or it will not answer the end. It is practical Atheism to reckon, that it exacts nothing more than to make me a passable citizen. If there were no God who is the righteous judge of all the earth, no tribunal of eternal justice, it would do well enough; but if there be both, where will many even of our justices and judges appear?

The Pharisees and scribes made egregrious mistakes even with the law in their hands and large inscriptions of it upon their dress. By fasting, praying and tything they supposed they were perfect, sinlessly perfect, but the great Lawgiver taught them better, that they neglected the weightier matters of the law, judgment, righteousness and the love of God. These ought ye to have done, and not to have left the other undone.

According to this incorrect way of expounding the law, Saul of Tarsus was blameless, when, but for his ignorance, he had committed the unpardonable sin in maliciously opposing the truth. When he became better versed in the true spirit of the law, he pronounces it holy and just and good; but says, I am carnal sold under sin. When the law came in its convictions and demands, menaces and terror, Sin revived, says he, and I died. We do not know how lively and strong sin is, until the law come with its just claims. Happy is it, however, for those who know something of the strength of sin, while they are near a stronger Saviour : happy they who die indeed unto sin, that they may live unto God. Having despaired in themselves, they are induced to hope in God, putting no confidence in the flesh. They see, with great astonishment, the love of God, in giving his Son for poor self destroyed sinners. " When we were without strength, in due time Christ died for the ungodly"—" For what the law could not do, in that it was weak through the flesh, God sent forth his own Son in the likeness of sinful flesh, and for sin condemned sin in the flesh, that the righteousness of the law might be fulfilled in us, who walk, not after the flesh, but after the Spirit." They will then reason with the Apostle, "If one died for all, then were all dead, that they who live should not henceforth live unto themselves, but unto Christ that died for them and rose again."

Thus—"The *law* of the Lord is perfect, converting the soul; the testimony of the Lord is sure, making wise the simple. The statutes of the Lord are right, rejoicing the heart: the *commandment* of the Lord is pure, enlightening the eyes. Psalm xix. 7, 8.

The law of God is useful in shewing us what we ought to be, holy in heart and in life. "Be ye holy," says God in the law, "for I am holy." The necessity, propriety and utility of this requisition wou'd never have been doubted, had we not by the fall become depraved as well as guilty. We were originally made after the image of God, in knowledge, righteousness and true holiness. The law of God would to us, continuing in that state, have been pleasant, natural and agreeable. In our fallen state it is not so. "The carnal mind is enmity against God, and is not subject to the *law* of God, neither indeed can be." To the regenerate, however, it is a glass in which they see genuine character and conduct reflected, and that every regenerate man will say, with the Apostle, "I delight in the law of God after the inward man." The gospel calls sinners, not

K 2

righteous and holy men ; but it does not call them to continuance in sin, but to repentance—we are called, not to sin, but to holiness. " But we are bound to give thanks always to God for you, brethren, beloved of the Lord, because God hath from the beginning chosen you to salvation through sanctification of the Spirit and belief of the truth. Whereunto he called you by our gospel to the obtaining of the glory of our Lord Jesus Christ." Thes. ii. 13, 14. " Follow peace with all men and holiness, without which no man shall see the Lord." This is the object of God the Father in our election, of God the Son in our redemption, and of God the Spirit in our sanctification. Eph. 1. 4. "According as he hath chosen us in him before the foundation of the world, that we should be *holy*, and without blame before him in love." 1 Pet. 1, 18. "Forasmuch as ye know that ye were not redeemed with corruptible things as silver and gold from your vain conversation received by tradition from your fathers ; but with the precious blood of Christ, as of a lamb without blemish and without spot." This redemption Jesus wrought, that he might present us faultless, without spot of pollution, or wrinkle of the old nature, and for this purpose he gives us of his holy spirit to take of the things that are his, and shew them unto us. This Holy Spirit sanctifies the redeemed of the Lord by the truth of the Lord. "Sanctify them through the truth : thy word is truth." John xvii. 17. Their high thoughts are brought low ; every imagination is brought into the obedience of faith, an obedience which the first commandment clearly requires. They are cleansed in their whole character, for that faith, by which they live, works by love, and purifies their heart. 1 Pet. 1, 22. 'Seeing ye have purified your souls, in obeying the truth, through the Spirit, unto unfeigned love of the brethren, see that ye love one another with a pure heart fervently." Contemplating these facts and principles, the believer will imitate the Apostle and say—"Not as though I had attained, either were already perfect: but I follow after, if that I may apprehend that, for which also I am apprehended of Christ Jesus. Brethren, I count not myself to have apprehended : but this one thing I do, forgetting the things which are behind, and reaching forth unto those things which are before, I press toward the mark, for the prize of the high calling of God in Christ Jesus." Phil. iii. 12, 13, 14. The law is so exceeding broad and spiritual, that, whatever be a man's previous attainments, he will, when he compares himself with this model, seem to have attained nothing. The Christian will therefore be humble and yet not despair. Encompassed about with so great a cloud of witnesses, he will lay aside every weight and the sin which doth most easily beset him and he will run, with patience, the race set before him. He will look to Jesus the Author and finisher of his faith. He will make mention of his righteousness, lean upon his strength and hope in his salvation; so will he run that he may obtain. He

will not, however, run at random—he will not
fight as those that beat the air.   He will have the
law of the Lord in his heart and in his hand, as
the guide of his conduct.   In perusing this, and
seeking the illumination of the Spirit, he will be
constantly saying, Lord what wouldst thou have
me to do ?   While faithful ministers preach to
such characters, they will confute all the calum-
nies of the adversaries, who charge gospel ministers with saying, " Let us continue in sin that
grace may abound."   They will shew in their
doctrine, and in the practice of t'eir people, that
they do not make void the *law* through faith, but
that they establish the law.   What ! sha'l we cor-
tinue in sin ?   Nay, how shall we, that are dead
to sin, live any longer therein ? This law will be
a delightful manual in their christian journey.
It will point out the duty of every relation and
every station of life.   Understanding it, and by
grace, walking according to it, they will have as
much comfort as if God was, in bodily shape,
walking with them, and showing them the road ;
or saying in an audible voice, " This is the way
walk ye in it."   Shall they not then, in keeping
his commandments, have a great reward ?   Hear
what he says to his disciples and through them
to all faithful ministers. Matth. xxviii. 19, 20.
"Go ye therefore, and teach all nations, baptizing
them in the name of the Father, and of the Son,
and of the Holy Ghost ; *teaching them to observe
all things whatsoever I have commanded you : and
lo, I am with you alway, even unto the end of the
world.* Amen."

The law not only *continues* in its *sanction*, but is in many respects, now in gospel times, more *strict*, and the violation of it more severely *punished* than in former times.

God requires of men obedience according to the opportunities they have of knowing his law. Thus "in times of ignorance, God winked at those things, but will now have all men every where to repent." " The servant, that transgresseth, not knowing his masters will, shall be beaten with few stripes ; but he that knoweth, and yet doeth it not, shall be beaten with many stripes. Sin is the transgression of the law. Were man then, so circumstanced, that he could know nothing about it, neither by natural or supernatural revelation, he would then be clear. " Where there is no law, there is no transgression : When the law is exhibited in its spirit, as well as in its letter in the gospel dispensation, the transgression of the law becomes far more criminal, and its *sanction* will be far more *terrible.*

Has Nineveh been judged for the sins of its inhabitants, when we can hardly find its scite ?

Have Tyre and Sidon, those wealthy mercantile cities, been punished, when fishermen dry their nets upon the rocks where once they stood.

Have Sodom Gomorrah and the cities of the plain been judged, when they were consumed by fire from heaven, and are now submersed with the noisome waters of the Dead sea ? Far more terrible judgments, however, await the cities of those nations who have enjoyed, and yet not

obeyed the gospel of Jesus .Christ.· He will
pour his fury upon the nations and upon the families that call not on his name. _He will turn all
nations into hell that forget God. Jer. x 25.
Psalm ix. 17. "Therefore we ought to give the
more earnest heed to the things which we have
heard, lest at any time we let them slip; for if the
word spoken by angels was steadfast, and every
transgression and disobedience received a just
recompence of reward, how shall we escape?
Heb. ii. 1, 2, 3. Has not the law received in the
sufferings of Christ the most awful sanction?
Though he was personally innocent and immacu-
lately pure, see how the sword of justice smote
Him when standing our surety. If the Almighty
supporter of all things groaned beneath the pres-
sure of the law's curse, when he stood the substitute of all believers, where would that curse
crush feeble reptiles? If such things were done
on the green tree, what will become of the dry?
Verily those who fall even upon the Rock of Salvation shall be broken, but those upon whom he
falls in terrible vengeance, he will grind them to
powder. Did the law thunder in its promulgation at Sinai?—how terrible must its sanction
be when it shall be executed in all its terrors upon
sinners at the last day? This will be peculiarly
terrible to those who have known, or had a gospel opportunity to know its principles. Hebrews
x, 26. "If we sin wilfully after that we have received the knowledge of the truth, there remaineth no more sacrifice for sin, but a certain fearful

looking for [of judgment, and fiery indignation
which shall devour the adversaries. He that despised Moses' law, died without mercy under two or
three witnesses. Of how much sorer punishment,
suppose ye, shall he be thought worthy, who hath
trodden under foot the Son of God," &c. To
cast light upon the *sanction of the law*, the heavens and the earth shall yet burn in awful blaze,
when the wrathful torch shall be put to the funeral pile of nature. 2 Pet. iii. 7. "For the heavens
and the earth which are now, by the same word
are kept in store, reserved unto fire against the
day of judgment, and perdition of ungodly men:
v. 10. But the day of the Lord will come as a
thief in the night; in the which the heavens shall
pass away with a great noise, and the elements
melt with fervent heat, the earth also, and the
works that are therein, shall be burned up. v. 11.
Seeing then that all these things shall be dissolved, what manner of persons ought ye to be in all
holy conversation and godliness? v. 12. Looking
for and hastening unto the coming of the day of
God, wherein the heavens being on fire shall be
dissolved," &c. Yes, let us hasten for he comes
to every one of us quickly. Rev. xxii. 12. "Behold I come quickly; and my reward is with me,
to give to every man according as his work shall
be. Then shall we see this saying verified. v. 14.
" BLESSED ARE THEY THAT DO HIS COMMAND-
MENTS, that they may have right to the tree of life,
and may enter in, through the gates, into the
city,"

PART IV.

The subjects and mode of Christian Baptism.

CHAP. I.

IN the discussion of this topic, we must, in the first place, remember that the Saviour of the Church is the Sovereign of the Church. Such therefore as are his servants and stewards must conduct the affairs of his house accordiag to his pleasure. In the second place, what is his pleasure must be learned from his own word.

There is no doubt but infinite wisdom, and perfect propriety mark all his arrangements. The modes of worship which he has prescribed, and modes of communicating his mind to his subjects, which he has adopted, do not form any exceptions. If the device of salvation, as a whole, could never have been conceived by any finite mind, it certainly ill becomes mortals to criticise upon its parts. The business of reason is, to draw fair conclusions from known and acknowledged facts. She is certainly, therefore, very much out of her place, when she says, another way would be better than that which revelation enjoins.

The scripture is not, formally, a confession of our faith ; nor yet a specific directory of our worship : yet it will be granted by all humble and pious disciples of Jesus Christ that it contains the only proper elements of both. Men are addressed as reasonable creatures, and ought, therefore, to consider carefully what is revealed to them for a rule of faith and practice. Men are addressed as rational creatures in the scriptures. 1 Cor. x. 15. "I speak as to wise men ; judge ye what I say." 1 Cor. xi. 13, 14. "Judge in yourselves ; is it comely that a woman pray unto God uncovered ? Doth not nature itself teach you"? Our great solicitude, therefore, in this matter and in all ordinances of worship should be to know and do the Master's revealed will.

It will in this as in every thing else be pleasant to know the reason of things, but still we must know that he is not bound to give us an account of his high doings and holy ways. Where reason, therefore, cannot clearly see, let her humbly adore. In her own province, i. e. where there is no specific direction given, and when the matter is cognizable by her powers, let reason preside. "Let every thing be done decently and in order." The Apostle directed the Christians at Phillipi to employ the principles of right reason, and taste to religious order. Phil. iv. 8. "Finally brethren, whatsoever things are true, whatsoever things are honest, whatsoever things are just, whatsoever things are pure, whatsoever things are lovely, whatsoever things are of good report ; if there be any virtue, and if there be any praise, think on these things." Attention to these principles of scripture, is necessary to keep us clear of extremes. On one side stands the Scylla of

L

formality; on the other the Charibdis of fanati.
cism : Against the danger of splitting on either
of these rocks we must look out, if we would
steer clear, and arrive safe in the harbor of
Truth.

. With regard to the character of adults who
should be baptised, there will be little controversy between Reformers and Regular Baptists.
We always opposed the practice of indiscriminate
administration of ordinances, and the practice of
the half way covenant, now very justly, and very
generally exploded. It is necessary that adult
applicants for baptism should be examined with
regard to their knowledge of the system of grace
and salvation generally. Those who are obviously yet in the kingdom of darkness, cannot,
with propriety, be admitted into the kingdom of
Christ by the badge of a religious profession.
In allusion to this principle the baptism of adults
used to be called by the Greeks, *photismos, illumination ;* and Paul, from whose eyes the scales
of ignorance fell, before his baptism, calls baptised persons, "once enlightened." Heb. vi. 4.
They must give evidence, that they cordially believe those truths which they intelligently know.
Philip first instructs the eunuch, and then he says,
" If thou believest with all thine heart thou
mayest." Acts viii. 36. It is very desirable to
see those, who apply for baptism, moved with
humble penitence, and holy contrition: "When
they heard this, they were *pricked in their hearts,*
and said unto Peter and to the rest of the Apos-

tles, "Men and brethren what shall we do." If
they have been enormously and notoriously sinners, they ought to give evidence that they are
disposed to break off their sins, by bringing forth
fruits becoming repentance. Speaking with divers tongues, or in languages never learned, and
other miraculous manifestations of the presence
of the Spirit of God, are not now ordinarily to be
expected. It would, however, be very desirable
to see evidence of his sanctifying influence in
their heart, upon their life and conversation. It
is unreasonable to expect that these evidences
should be so distinct in new converts, as they
ought to be in old and *experienced* Christians.
Converts have their stages of progress and growth
in grace and holiness. There is grace in the
blade, in the ear, and in the full grown, and mature grain in the ear. The evidence of grace in
its earliest stage ought to be considered enough
to recommend its subject and possessor to the enjoyment of the privilege of baptism. "Him that
is weak in the faith receive ye, but not to doubtful disputation." Rom. xiv. 1. It is very evident from this, that a person may be a proper subject of Chris tian baptism, and yet not be prepared
for the participation of the Lord's supper. Every member of the family must have food, but it
should be food appropriate and suited to his years
and strength. The new born babe will desire,
and ought to have, the sincere milk of the word
for nourishment and satisfaction ; the more advanced in years will be occasionally admitted to

feast at the table with the seniors of the family, yea with the Lord of the house.

It would be cruel to allow any to participate in this ordinance, who have not a perception of its mysteries. Even the children of God may partake unworthily of the supper, and instead of nourishing the spiritual life, may eat and drink judgment even to the extinction of the natural life. 1 Cor. xi. 30. Not so in regard of the former, when we see evidence of the presence and power of the Holy Ghost, we may say with Peter Acts x. 47. "Can any forbid water, that these should not be baptised, which have received the Holy Ghost as well as we?" This text clearly confutes the idle cavils of those who argue against water baptism, as they in derision call it. How contradictory is this reasoning to that of the Apostle? They say it is no matter about water baptism, if we have the baptism of the Spirit. The Quaker reasons too, that there can be no water baptism, if we admit a baptism of the Spirit, because there is but one baptism. His mistake arises out of his ignorance of the nature of a sacrament which, though one, has two parts, the external and symbolical, and the internal, spiritual and real. Now it is true, that men can be saved by the latter, without the former, and not by the former without the latter. The penitent thief was admitted with the Saviour into Paradise, without the participition of any sacrament. Judas eat the last passover with our Lord, and yet was the son of perdition, and went to his own place. Simon was baptised with Apostolic hands, and yet was in the gall of bitterness and bond of iniquity. On the other hand it is very plain, that no intelligent Christian will despise the institutions of divine grace, which are so admirably adapted to our case and character—so well calculated to represent, seal, and apply, by the blessing of God's Spirit, the benefits of Christ's purchase to his heritage and people.

To say that ordinances save, is to idolize them; to say they may be neglected with innocence or impunity, is to despise the wisdom and goodness of God, and to proclaim our own ignorance, arrogance and impiety.

Of this, however, we must say no more at present, but proceed to consider, Whether infants are proper subjects of Christian baptism? When we enquire if infants are proper subjects of baptism, we do not mean any infants. We agree with Anti-Pedobaptists thus far, that the children of Heathens and scandalous or ungodly professors are to be excluded until they profess their faith in Christ and obedience to him; but we also say that the infants of such, as are members of the visible Church, are to be baptized.

The first principle upon which we plead the right of infants to membership in the Church, is their ancient and unrepealed charter. They were, as we have already seen in treating of the covenant with Abraham, and the law, publicly recognized. If they must not be so now, we want to know the reason of this rejection. Has

L 2

their right to membership been recalled ?   If it
has been recalled, where is that transaction recorded ? where is the repeal ? This would require
to be very explicit on many accounts. First.
Because it is a common usage among nations
that the son be considered a member of the same
commonwealth or kingdom, of which his father is
a member.   In taking the census or list of inhabitants and citizens in any corporation the children are not excluded.   This practice is not an
innovation of modern times.   It is a practice as
ancient as the history of social man.   God himself sanctions the use of it in regard to the city of
Nineveh ?   Jonah 4, 11. "And should not I
spare Nineveh, tha· great city, wherein are more
than sixscore thousand persons that cannot discern between their right hand and their left
hand."   Here you see we have, in round numbers, a list of the young population of this great
ancient city.   These unconscious babes too, were
the citizens for whose sake God pleads with the
peevish prophet that the city should be spared.
Why then, the man of reading and reflection will
ask, Why are children not included among the
members of the commonwealth of the Church ?
Why are they not considered citizens of the New
Testament, as well as of the Old Testament Sion ?
Why are they not according to uniform custom
considered members of the kingdom of heaven as
well as their parents ? Is there any case in
which children are not accounted legitimate heirs
of such social privileges as belonged to their par-

ents'? Why was Paul a Roman citizen? He never purchased that freedom; he never swore an oath of allegiance to that government to obtain that franchise; " Ay, but he was free born." Well, and are we prepared to say that the Roman empire was more generous and kind to its infant population than the Redeemer's empire is? Shall the fourth beast of Daniel's vision, which was "exceeding dreadful, whose teeth were of iron and his nails of brass, which devoured and brake in pieces, and stamp the residue with his feet," Dan. vii. 19—Shall this beast of prey be more kind to his children born in Tarsus, than the Lamb, on mount Sion to the children born in his city Jerusalem?

We know men otherwise very respectable, will go far in maintaining a cause which they have once taken up. But let that, for a moment, be forgotten, and see if every candid, generous and pious mind would not revolt at the thought of such an impeachment. What! the sensible soul would exclaim, shall we make the ancient of days, the Judge of all the earth more cruel than the ostrich? Shall we suppose that he who is about to set up a righteous and an everlasting kingdom, that he will exclude infants from it?—that he who was himself the *child born* and the Son given will, from that corporation, of which, in an eminent degree he carries the keys, lock out the children of his people? All this, however, that system most evidently does, which denies the children of believing and pious parents the right of membership in the Church. Is there any man, untrammelled by system and sophism, who does not see the inconsistency of this?

Second. If the ancient right of membership in, the Church has been recalled, the repeal of that important clause in the charter would need to be particularly explicit, to satisfy the believing Jew. He had been well acquainted with the application of this representative principle, not only in the state, but also in the Church, in the ancient administration. He was feelingly alive to any alteration from his old customs. This principle he carried even to servile bigotry and attachment to onerous rites of the typical service. The Redeemer of Israel bestowed pains to emancipate the minds of his ancient people from such bondage. He shews them that he has now, for ever, by one sacrifice perfected all them that are sanctified. If there had been a change made in this particular, i. e. If infants, that used to be members of the Church in the wilderness, according to the tenor of that covenant which was confirmed of God in Christ with Abraham, were now excluded when the Seed appeared, is it possible, on the supposition of such a change being made, that the Jew would make no enquiry, and that the King of the Jews and Prophet of Israel would, neither by himself, nor by his Apostles, give any solution of such a difficult problem? Parents are generally tender of their infants and scrupulous of maintaining their rights. Had, therefore, the administrators of the gospel in the early establishment of Christianity, told the Jewish proselytes that their children could, by no rite, be received into the Church, you may rely upon it we would have heard something about it. We hear nothing, however; we therefore fairly conclude that no such thing was done—that the charter of ancient privilege to their children was ratified; that they received the initiatory seal of covenant privilege in the Church along with their parents. The silence of the Jew on this subject is a known and acknowledged fact, if there be any other possible, or even plausible, way of accounting for it, we want our opponent to adduce it; if there be not, he must acquiesce in this fair inference, that the question was never agitated by the Apostles and ministers of the primitive Church. But if this question was not agitated, doubtless infants were accounted members of the Church and received the initiatory seal, or badge of membership. If they who joined from the Jewish race, received the privilege of baptism for their children, why should not the Gentiles? are not Jews and Gentiles all one in Christ Jesus? If Jews and Gentiles both received this privilege for their children in the early period of the Christian era, when was this privilege withdrawn? Who had a right, since that period, to abridge the privileges of the members of Christ's mystical body—the Church?

Third. This principle will gather strength in its application to the point in hand, if we consider this known fact, viz. that in general the adminis-

tration of the covenant of grace, since the advent
and suffering of Christ, has been more obviously
liberal and gracious than before.   Although as
we have seen, there was grace in the legation of
Moses, yet so far does the grace of this dispensation excel that that is eclipsed. "The law was
given by Moses. Grace and truth came by Jesus Christ."   John 1. 17.   The law, even when
dealing out threats in its most legal, literal and
killing form speaks of "visiting the iniquities of
the fathers upon the children unto the third and
fourth generation of them that hate me, and shewing mercy unto thousands (generations) of them
that love me and keep my commandments."
Did not this threat and this promise shine with
weighty lustre from Sinai ? and are children now
to be altogether neglected and unknown ?   No.
ii. Cor. iii. 9, 10. " For if the ministration of
condemnation be glory, much more doth the ministration of righteousness exceed in glory.   For
even that which was made glorious, had no glory
in this respect, by reason of the glory that excel-
leth."   Are females now known in society—are
Gentiles of every tribe now called to enjoy the
privileges of the Church?   Are the rites of religion less operous and expensive, yet more evangelical, clear and expressive ? Is the administration of the gracious covenant of salvation in every
respect more benign than ever before ?   How is
it then that infants are excluded, now, seeing they
were not before ?   Every considerate man before
he can believe that infants are now excommuni-

cated from the Church must have exceedingly, clear evidence that their ancient rights have been revoked : the thing itself is so very unlikely, and improbable, so obviously incongruous with the other parts of this dispensation. What ! if this revocation has taken place it cannot be in mercy. It was in mercy that God said, " I will be the God of your seed." It cannot, therefore, be in mercy and grace that he would say, I will *not* be the God of your seed any longer. Is it then in judgment ? These are to be sure judgments inflicted on the great body of the Jews according to their own terrible imprecation. "His blood be on us and on our children." But this blood is not on the head of those who believe: No ! For them he prayed, " Father forgive them, they know not what they do." Why then should not their children with their parents revert to their wonted immunities and privileges?

Thus it is evident the man of common sense, from the rational principles of his nature—the politician from ordinary principles of jurisprudence—the philosopher from observation on the ways of Providence—the Jew from what he had. been taught in the past dispensations of mercy— the Christian, enlightened by the special radiancy and brightness of the gospel, all, all would expect that children should be recognized as members of the same corporation of the parents. They would expect that the infants of such as are members of the visible Church should be baptized. Are they then taught otherwise by the

Saviour of the Gentile as well as of the Jew ?
If they are then, let every imagination be brought·
into subjection to the obedience of faith. Let
reason knuckle to revelation ; but let revelation
be reasonably examined. With this view let the
candid reader consult the motto of our plea.
Math. xix. 14. " Jesus said, suffer little children
and forbid them not to come unto me, for of such
is the kingdom of heaven." When we read any
part of the scriptures we should have our ears
open to hear what God speaks. Men's thoughts
may be very pretty and considerably impressive,
but there is an unction and a profundity in all divine revelation which defies all successful imitation. This we may say is eminently the case
when Jesus, who spake as never man, is the
speaker. What then is this passage intended to
teach ? Were these children affected with dis-
eases and maladies which their parents wished to
have healed ? Of bodily maladies the passage
hints nothing. We can hardly suppose that the
disciples would be so grossly inhumane or unbelieving as to have rebuked the parents for bringing them to him who had proved himself often in·
their sight to be, even for the body, the great·
Physician. The occult qualities and constitu-
tional nature of infantile; the inveteracy and confirmed habit of senile disease, which frequently
eludes the skill, and baffles the powers of human·
doctors, had often been demonstrated to be quite·
sanable by this Divine Healer. The reply then·
does not seem to intimate that this was the object,

the parents wished to obtain, or the disciples to hinder. What, we again ask, is the passage designed to teach? If it mean nothing more than that children may be saved, this would imply that the disciples denied and wished to oppose the salvation of infants. This had indeed been a horrid sentiment, more cruel than ever held by the wildest sect of men. The disciples would have shuddered at the suggestion, that the Saviour would not show his condescension in the salvation of infants. This then cannot be a reproof of their illiberality in that respect and to that degree. The true history of the case seems to have been some how thus. The parents conceived a very high opinion of Jesus the Saviour; they wished the infants in their arms, and the little children that clung by the skirts of their garments, to partake of his divine benediction. The Saviour approved of their faith; he rejoiced in beholding the heart cheering scene, and in manifesting his condescension to, and care of, the lambs. He saw some there that he knew were to be eminent by his grace in the Church. Nicephorus tells us, that the famous father Ignatius was one of the babes now presented to Jesus for his reception and blessing. The disciples seem to have been left to fall, for a little, into this unbelieving, carnal and proud-way of reasoning. These parents and children are encroaching upon our master's time and more important business of instructing and proselyting adults. They seem strangely to have fallen into the system of Anti-pedobaptists,

M

and so to have concluded, that any public relig-.
ious attention to babes was useless, seeing they
did not understand the use of it. Such seems
obviously to have been the view of the disciples,
in thrusting away the parents who came to put
their children into the arms of Jesus. Strange
there are parents by pious instinct wishing to do
their duty, and active to fulfil a prophecy, and
there are teaching disciples that for a time oppose both. What! did they not know that the
great Shepherd, whose voice they heard and followed, was to *gather the lambs in his arms?* All
events of Providence subserve the system of
grace. Those who act in concurrence and those
who act in opposition seem frequently alike ignorant of this.

The instruction of the scripture, while it has a
particular adaptation to the case on which it was
first exhibited, has a practical accommodation to
a whole class of analagous cases. Had there not
been a propriety at this time to reprove the Anti-
pedobaptist spirit of the disciples, the children
could, as well, have been blessed at a distance as
at hand. The design then of the saying of our
Lord is to teach us all, that in some public way
children should be presented to Christ, and acknowledged as members of the kingdom of heav-
en or of his Church.

I do not see how our opponents will avoid this
conclusion, except by saying, either, that they
were not children, in age, but in grace ; or by
saying, that the kingdom does not mean the

Church. As to the first, viz. that they were not children in age, but in grace, by a new, and not by a natural birth ;—in answer to this we would confidently say, that if they were not children in age, it would be hard to shew what words or circumstance would be calculated to express such. First. The word is the diminutive of child, it is *paidion* our translators noticed this and so calls them *little* children. In the parallel passage, Luke xviii. 15, they are called *brephe*, " And they brought unto him *infants*, that he should teach them, and when the disciples saw it, they rebuked them." This name is given to those who are passive or considerably in receiving their food. It is sometimes used for a babe in its mother's womb. Luke 1, 41. " When Elizabeth heard the salutation of Mary *the babe* [*brephe*] leaped in her womb." Sometimes for a new born child. Luke 11, 12. " Ye shall find the babe wrapped in swaddling clothes." The farthest that it can go in expressing age is when the child first begins to receive the affectionate lessons of a parent. 2 Tim. iii. 15. " And that from a child thou hast known the scriptures." Second. The circumstances ; parents bring them. It is to the parents that the reproof of the disciples is directed. Mark x. 13. " And they brought young children to him that he should touch them, and his disciples rebuked *those that brought* them " It is true it is said suffer them to come, but who does not know that we speak in this style of every person or thing approaching us, whether it be active or passive. How often have we all heard one kind matron addressing the child of another before it could speak or stand, " Come to me." Again, as we have already hinted, it is quite likely that some of them were walking and some of them sucking children. Concerning all of them it is said that he took them up in his arms. Mark x. 16. " And he took them up in his arms, put his hands upon them and blessed them." The very circumstance, that the disciples opposed their access to Christ, will be strong as a thousand arguments to every attentive reader, that these were children in age. Would it not seem passing strange indeed that the disciples, who, with the exception of Judas Iscariot, have been always accounted regenerated men, and were acquainted with the fact that except a man was born again he could not enter into the kingdom of heaven, should object to their admission on this very account. That Servetus, who ridiculed the doctrine of the Trinity, and argued that infants should not be baptized, because the doctrines of Trismegistus and the Sibyls forbade sacred ablutions to any but adults, should so explain the passage as to involve such an absurdity, need not seem strange. That men who are ignorant and unlearned, should wrest the scriptures need not surprise us. From those who have no recommendation to teach but that they say they are converted and called, we are not to look for consistency. But that such men as Dr. Gill of London, and Dr. Stoughton of Philadelphia, should countenance and circulate such inept comments on sacred scripture is really astonishing. It shews how far even men of learning may go in defending a favorite system.

Farther—If we make one part of the passage allegorical, we must make the other so also. Make the children, then, not children of age, but in grace; then who will be the parents? Who was it that begat men by the word of truth, and travailed as in birth until Christ was formed within them? Was it not the disciples? Then according to this the disciples would be the parents presenting them, and opposed to their presentation at the same time.

But, will it be said, as a dernier resort, that the children presented were children in years? but that when he says, of such are the kingdom of heaven, he means those who are made such by grace? We admit, that unless a man be converted and become as a little child in docility and dependance upon the heavenly Father, he cannot be saved. chap. xviii. 3. Every regenerate person becomes, in many respects, as a little child; but, if this be the construction, the disciples might say, All this is admitted, but it is not to the point. Shall we then charge a *non sequitur* to a proposition of our Lord. Every person must see this gloss of the passage would make the Saviour's position inconclusive. That, therefore, cannot be the meaning of the Saviour's remark. Try it. Suffer these little children to come unto me, and forbid them not; for of grown up, regenerate persons is the kingdom of heaven. One would suppose that even party prejudice would feel a little reluctant, at putting such an incoherent argument into the mouth of the divine Teacher.

It may be thought, however, in the second place, that these absurdities may be evaded by saying that the phrase, *kingdom of heaven*, means the place and state of endless happiness, or the Church above. But this is not only contrary to the general current of expositors and the scope of the place itself, it would also be not a little odd, if they could be members of the church of glory, and yet could not belong to the church of grace —of the church triumphant and not of the church militant. If they may be admitted members of the heavenly society, would it not be proper that, by some ordinance, their obligation to the blood of atonement should be expressed? Our Baptist brethren, of the regular order, at least, we, hope, are not become Socinians to deny original sin, nor heathens, to think of any other way of salvation, but by the name of Jesus. The passage then plainly proves that children in age should be al-

and should, by regular church officers, be acknowl-edged members of his Church. If so, we ask, By what rite? Let the Baptists themselves answer. They practically admit that baptism is the rite whereby membership in the Church is declared or effected. It will avail nothing here to say, that these children were not baptized. The adults whom Christ received, he did not baptize, *for he baptized none* (John iv. 2) nor was baptism as yet perfectly settled as the door of admission ; but he did that which was tantamount; he invited them to him, encouraged the bringing of them, and signified to his disciples, to whom the keys of the kingdom of God were given, that they were members of his kingdom ; and accordingly conferred upon them the blessings of that kingdom : and his giving them the thing signified may sufficiently justify his ministers in giving the sign.

In other societies, the children of such as are members are commonly looked upon as members. Though a wise man doth not always beget a wise man, yet a free man begets a free man. As the pious Matthew Henry justly remarks—" The king of England would give those small thanks, who should cut off all the children of the kingdom. Our law calls natural allegiance, *high allegiance*, and he that oweth it is called *subditus natus*, natural liege subject. It is the privilege of the subject, and the prerogative of the king, that it should be so." And shall it not be allowed in the visible kingdom of Christ? By the Jewish law, if a servant married and had children born in the master's house, they were the master's ; they were taken under his protection and interested in the privileges of the family, though yet capable of no service. This law David applies spiritually. Psalm cxvi. 16. *O Lord, truly I am thy servant; I am thy servant, the son of thy handmaid, born in thy house.* Those consult neither the honour of the master, the credit of the family, nor the benefit of their children, who, though servants in Christ's family themselves, will not allow their children. To deny the Church membership of the seed of believers, is to deny privileges to those who once had them, and who have never forfeited them. It is, in effect, to deliver their children to Satan as members of his visible kingdom; for I know no mean between the kingdom of darkness and the kingdom of light. Give me leave, then, as the infants' advocate, to make their complaint in the words of David, 1 Sam. xxvi. 19. *They have driven me out this day from abiding in the inheritance of the Lord, saying, Go and serve other gods,* and to present their petition for a visible church membership, in the words of the Reubenites and Gadites. Josh. xxii. 24, 25—*For fear lest, in time to come your children might speak unto our children, saying, What have you to do with the Lord God of Israel; ye have no part in the Lord; so shall your children make our children cease from fearing the Lord.* Therefore, according to the warrant of the written word, we maintain baptism, as a sign of the church membership of our infants; *that it may be a witness for our generations after us, that they may do the service of the Lord, and might not be cut off from following after him.* For whatsoever those who are otherwise minded, uncharitably suggest, *the Lord God of Gods, the Lord God of gods, he knoweth and Israel shall know, that it is not in rebellion nor transgression against the Lord.* We desire to express as great a jealousy as they can do for the institutions of Christ, and are as fearful of going. a step without a warrant.

Several other scriptural arguments, have been undeniably. urged, to prove the church member. ship of infants ; but what was said to prove their covenant right, and to shew the reasons of it, serve indifferently to this ; for the visible church and the external administration of the covenant are of equal extent and latitude. Grant me that infants are of that visible body, or society, to *which pertaineth the adoption and the glory & the covenant,* &c. in the same sense, in which these pertained to the Jews of old and to their seed; and I desire no more. That is their covenant right, and their church membership which enti- tleth them to baptism.

We have before said, that Christ had not, at the time in which he took up these children in his arms and blessed them, appointed baptism as the badge of his disciples. That institution was not to be generally observed, until after his baptism unto death ;. and therefore, he does not institute it until recently before his passion. Let us con- sider the words of institution. Matth. xxviii. 19. " Go ye, therefore, teach all nations, baptising them in the name of the Father, and of the Son, and of the Holy Ghost." The word rendered, *teach,* in the former part of this verse is not the same of that which is translated, *teach,* in the be- ginning of the next verse. The former is *mathe•*

teusate ; the latter is *didaskontes.* The distinction of their meaning is as great as of their form
and ought to be observed. The first is a causative verb, formed from the word which signifies
a disciple, and so its meaning is evidently to dis-
cipulate or make disciples, i. e. initiate them into
the school of the Church. In all cases children
are introduced as scholars before they are taught.
Students are matriculated before they enjoy the
advantages of seminaries of learning. So it is to
be done here. Disciple the nations, baptizing
them, i. e. Disciple them by this rite. It is well
known that infants compose a great part of all
nations ; the general command, therefore will embrace all the particular characters. It was not
necessary to say, men, women and children. All
these were evidently included in the general term
nations. If they had been unacquainted with
the ancient plan and common order of society—
with the particular condescension and kindness
of Christ to babes, it might have been necessary
that some specification should have been made.
The disciples, however, were supposed to be men
of common sense, and had received in the school
of Jesus instruction to qualify them for their
work. All that can be inferred from the circumstance that (*matheteusate*) disciple precedes the
word baptise is, that they were to be in the way of
learning. Now who does not know that parents
may bind children to trades, employ for them
tutors, confer upon them rights, and leave them
inheritances before they are of age ? All this

should be done under proper responsible guardians.

Suppose the dispensation had been altered solely with respect to the extent of character whom it would embrace; and not with respect to the mode and rites of administration. Instead of being sent exclusively to the lost sheep of the house of Israel, let them be sent to all the nations of the earth to proselyte and circumcise. Would they in this case, have needed any particular instruction respecting the infants of their proselytes? Would they not have known that the descendants of such as believed and became members of the church, whose usage on that point had been long known should be circumcised? If they had neglected this would there have been no Jew or Gentile convert, acquainted with Jewish statute and precedent upon that subject, who would have said, Why are our children excluded when we are received? We have been taught that this was a dispensation of peculiar mercy; why then are not children recognized and made visibly to participate of this mercy as well as before? What is the difference then between the cases? The disciples evidently understood the one coming in the room of the other, at least this far, that the one was the Jewish and the other the Christian rite of introduction into the Church.

It is to be observed also, that those who were commissioned were Jews, and needed not to be informed of the ancient usage of the church upon this subject, and if they had any unbelieving

scrup'e about the right of infants to membership
in his Church, and kingdom, he had already settled that in a passage previously considered and
adduced.

From this commission then it would appear
pretty clear that the Apostles and their successors
could have no reasonable scruples about admitting the infants of professors into the Church.
The rite of admission was baptism ; they, therefore, could have no scruple about baptizing the
infants of believers or members of the Church.
If they had been so illiberal and ill acquainted
with the Christian dispensation of eminent condescension and grace, they would have been corrected. Pious parents would have urged their
babes for admittance and the Redeemer would
plead their cause. To all this reasoning upon
the commission and original instruction given to
the Apostles, it may perhaps be objected, that although they are commanded to proselyte nations
[ta ethna] yet they are only commanded to baptize them, [autous] which Dr. Gill thinks is a
clear proof that them does not relate to nations
as its antecedent. Nations we admit is neuter in
the original and them masculine. But according
to his way of criticising, it is evident that females
would be excluded from this ordinance by the
commission ; but we know they are not by the
practice of the Apostles. Campbell says—
" There are manifestly three things which our
Lord here distinctly enjoins his Apostles to execute with regard to the nations, to wit—mathe-

tuein, baptizein, didaskein, that is, to convert them to the faith, to initiate the converts into the church by baptism, and to instruct the baptized in all the duties of the christian life." He shews a great many ways of rendering the first word matheteusate, and all his authorities agreeing on the meaning of the latter. Perhaps, however, it might be more proper to consider the charge as one thing, but the execution of it to consist of two parts. The charge is, make disciples of the nations. This is to be done by baptizing and teaching them. If you attend to the translation, it will shew you that this is the true meaning of it, and how well this will agree with the admission of infant pupils, every considerate person will at once see. It will not follow from this reasoning that the infants of Jews, Turks, and profane persons are to be baptized. These are not proselyted or converted. The Apostles would never once dream of such a thing; these parents would by no means allow it; and nothing but a desperate case would ever have made the Baptists suggest it as inferable. Infants have not yet learned the knowledge of Christ: that does not hinder their being members of the Christian's school. It would be a strange seminary, that would admit none as pupils but those who knew the very science, which it proposed to teach. It is evident from Rabbinical writings and from the scripture, that an unlearned person may be a Christian pupil. The Jewish children were considered members of that Church and nation, al-

N

though, as yet, they knew nothing of the constitution of either church or state. There is an account upon record of a Gentile who says to Rabbi Hillel; "*Fac me proselytum ut me doceas.*" *Make me a disciple or proselyte that you may teach me.*

It is very evident that if objections should be made to the foregoing as alluding to Jewish maxims, that we have these sanctioned and the point in hand established by New Testament authority. Acts xv. 10. " Now therefore, why tempt ye God, to put a yoke upon the neck of the *disciples*, which neither our fathers nor we were able to bear ?" It is evident here that circumcision is the matter of controversy. " Certain men came down from Judea and taught the brethren, Except ye be circumcised, after the manner of Moses, ye cannot be saved." " But there arose up certain of the sect of the Pharisees which believed saying, That it was needful to circumcise them and to command them to keep the law of Moses." This was quite natural that even those who believed of the Jews should have scruples about their ancient rituals. If they thought circumcision should continue in use it is impossible to shew, upon what-principle, they would reject infants from being its subjects. These men from Judea and the believing Pharisees, it appears, then wished to have circumcision administered to all who personally or by representation were members of Christ's school, i. e. adults and their infants. But these, upon whom they wished to impose this yoke are called *disciples*; therefore infants may be called disciples ; and if disciples, they may and ought to be baptised according to the words of institution. It will, perhaps, yet be objected against these conclusions, that the words here in Matthew must be taken in connection with the same commission as recorded in the other gospels, from which some infer, that faith is necessary in all cases to precede baptism.

We readily admit that before any adult person receive this ordinance, he should give evidence that he believes with all his heart. But it will never do to apply the same rules to infants as to adults. According to that mode of proceeding, you would starve your children to death and exclude them from all hopes of everlasting life. The commandment is peremptory. 2 Thes. iii. 10. "For even when we were with you, this we commanded you, that if any would not work neither should he eat." Now I cannot see, if we will apply rules to infants which evidently respect adults, why this *canon* would not forbid us to give children food as well as the commanding of faith and repentance, as prerequisites to adult baptism, would exclude them from that ordinance. Yea, it would be more exclusive only for the common sense and natural affection which commonly govern in natural things. The command about eating and drinking is negative and so peculiarly strong. "If any would not work, neither should he eat." That is manifestly much stronger than the other ; " Repent and be baptised. He that

believeth and is baptized; it is not—He that believeth not shall not be baptized. Are we then
to say, because our babes cannot work, that they
shall have no food? Verily this would exhibit
dark prospects of the duration and continuance of
the species in the world, as the exclusion of babes
from membership would do of the Church.

But, moreover, apply this rule a little farther,
and you will not only have none of them in the
Church below, but you will also shut against them
the gates of the Church above. Although it is
not said he that believeth not shall not be baptized, it is said "He that believeth not shall be
damned." Now, it is evident according to the
way our opponents argue, that infants cannot be
saved. Apply the adult rule to infant subjects,
and you see what horrid conclusions force themselves upon you. The Anabaptist reasons—Because the infant cannot believe, therefore it cannot be baptised. By a much clearer inference it
might be said, because they cannot believe, they
cannot be saved. It must be here observed that
I do not blame the Baptist for holding either of
these opinions, to wit : that children should be
starved ; or that they will all be excluded the
kingdom of heaven. It is their system and not
their hearts, that holds both of these shocking tenets. They would, in humanity, administer food
to the hungry babe—they would, in pity, pray
that babes might, in divine mercy be saved. It
would be but reasonable, however, to consider
consequences and renounce systems, which, if

followed, would be so horrid in their results. We have seen then that infants may be disciples, that those who are made disciples in the Church are to be baptized, that the tendency of the reasoning which opposes this, would lead to the starvation of children and the denial of their salvation. No scripture rightly understood can lead to absurdity, and scripture should be compared with scripture, before we draw inferences and conclusions, which we would not ourselves with their whole train admit.

Let us see then what other parts of holy writ will say upon this subject. Before we finally decide upon this interesting question, whether or not infants should be baptized, we must try what way the Apostles understood their instruction. We cannot do this better than by noticing their practice under this general direction. We have not any instance of a nation becoming Christian during the ministry of inspired men. Of course we have no Apostolic model for regulating a national Church.

Several years, yea centuries of years had to elapse from that period, before the kingdoms of the world should become the kingdoms of our Lord and of his Christ. However, they made full proof of their ministry. They labored to bring about the much desired time. They endeavored to compel men to enter into the kingdom. We have no instance of their ever refusing to baptize the infants of professors—no instance, after the regular establishment of the

Church in any place, that the children of adult members upon growing up, were baptized. We have very strong evidence that they did, under the direction of their permanent commission, baptize the infants of believing proselytes. What evidence ought to be required upon this head? Would it not be sufficient, if we had the ancient promise confirmed and ratified in connection with the command to receive this seal? Indeed only for the slowness of man's heart to believe, there would have been no necessity to confirm and ratify a divine grant. The heavens may depart and the earth be removed, but he will never fail of any thing he has promised. We might therefore have said, If he has not withdrawn his promise from the children; but we are not under the necessity of reasoning closely to maintain their right; we have line upon line and promise upon promise. To illustrate and prove our point let us suppose an instance:

Suppose a king possessed of large territories entirely at his own disposal, should first have enfeoffed his land to the adults and infants of a certain tribe. This enfeoffment is made by a seal attached to a charter. The original occupants forfeit their right, and by their rebellion alienate the property. After some time he alters the seal, and extends his royal munificence to all other tribes indiscriminately, upon their agreeing to come and be orderly residents in the region. He sends out factors and agents to seal and deliver over legal rights to the new settlers. Would any person suppose that the children, in this new arrangement were to be excluded? Certainly not. If some agents were afterwards to refuse this, would not the settlers have a right to enquire into the reason of the alteration. If none could be given but such as might, with equal propriety, have been advanced against the ancient, known custom and regulation of the tenure ; would not all think that these agents did not understand the nature of their lord's grant ?

The case, you will see, is similar to the one in hand. Examine Acts ii. 39. " For the promise is unto you and to your children, and to all that are afar off, even as many as the Lord our God shall call." The first of these characters are the descendants of Abraham, unto whom and to his seed the promise was originally given. The second, are the nations who are to be blessed in his seed, chap. iii. 25. " Ye are the children of the prophets and of the covenant which God made with our fathers saying to Abraham, And in thy seed shall all the nations of the earth be blessed." The promise can be no other than what we have been already considering in the second part of our plea, to wit, " I will be your God and the God of your seed." But this promise was sealed. Abraham received the sign of circumcision a *seal* of the righteousness of faith. His seed also received the seal. Male infants were to be circumsised. This promise is mentioned, confirmed and ratified in connection with a command to respect the seal and sacrament of baptism. This

itself is no obscure hint that baptism came in the
room of circumcision and should, of course, like
its predecessor be administered to infants, unless
you would make the type more condescending
and kind to babes than the antitype. Peter had
charged home upon the awakened consciences of
some, the terrible deed of crucifying the Lord.
They cried under pungent conviction, "Men and
brethren, what shall we do? Then Peter said
unto them, Repent and be baptized every one of
you in the name of Jesus Christ, for the remission of sins, and ye shall receive the gift of the
Holy Ghost."

In the verse already quoted, he assigns this as
a reason, " For the promise is unto you and to
your children." Why should children be here
mentioned, if they have nothing to do with the
promise nor its seal? It is trifling to say that
the promise would be to their children, when they
were grown up to be men and women, i. e. when
they are no longer children. It is evident that,
according to this way of explaining, or rather,
wresting the passage, there is no promise to
children. It is further added, lest any should be
led to believe that the Gentiles should not have
the same privileges; " And to all that are afar
off, even as many as the Lord our God shall call."
If none but adults have an interest in this promise, it will mangle and destroy the promise itself.
The promise is, " I will be the God of *your seed*,
as well as I will be your God." The promise
then was not according to its original form to

them, if not also to their infant seed. No person has any right to abstract from the grant of Jehovah. Our plea then is fair, that the promise is to the children of the called Gentiles, although anciently afar off, they are now brought nigh by the blood of Christ. They are no longer strangers, but fellow-citizens with the saints, and of the household of faith.

Shall they, then, who have the promise, not have the seal of the promise? Shall they of the household of faith, not have the privileges of that house or family? Shall citizens not have the immunities and franchise of citizens? What if the children of the Gentiles were once accounted stones, no matter if, by an enlargement of the grant, they are now accounted children, shall they not have the mark and name of children?

We have therefore seen that the Apostles gave these penitent applicants ground to expect, that, although the character of the seal was a little changed, still the same persons as formerly should receive it. Who were these? Were they not believing penitents and their children? Is it not, therefore, reasonable to suppose that believers would bring their children with them to be initiated, as formerly, into the same covenant privileges and state with themselves? Is there any hint, that in all these plausible calculations they were disappointed? What can be assigned as the reason that there is no such hint, unless it be the reason which establishes our plea, and the claim of the infants of church members to church

privileges, that is, that they were not disappointed in these calculations ?   But it will be said that
these were men, and had not their households
with them.   That this objection might be obvi-
ated, we have documents still more explicit upon
this head.   It will, therefore, be satisfactory to all
who love God's grace and the rights of children
founded thereon, if it be evident that the Apos-,
tles actually did baptize households.   It is well
known that house or household generally signifies families consisting of persons of different
ages, of adults and infants.   Now although there
are some houses in which there are no children ;
so there are some houses in which there are no
grown persons, still it is certain, that the word
house, when any moral act is done by, or upon it,
intimates that there are inhabitants, yea unless
there be something said to the contrary, that
there are children.

In this style of language the scripture often
speaks, " He maketh the barren woman to keep
house." Psalm cxiii. 9.   The explanation of that
phrase is given in the second part of the paral-
lelism, according to the idiom of Hebrew poesy
" and to be a joyful mother of children."   Thus
you see she is not considered properly to keep
house, until she is made a mother of children.
Take another instance of this signification of
house as certainly implying children. Jer. xi. 10.
" The *house* of Israel and the *house* of Judah have
broken my covenant, which I made with their fathers.", This text proves two things for our pur-.

pose.. 1st. That house signifies an assemblage of people of different ages. 2d. That posterity may be bound by the representation of their predecessors and fathers. If they were not bound by the covenant which God made with their fathers, how could they break its obligations?

Baptists themselves understand both of these principles. They understand the philological principle respecting the meaning of the word, as you may see by the way they sometimes reason on Ex. xii. 3, 4. They understand its moral principle. They consider treaties obligatory upon the posterity of the personal contractors. Should it be said that *house* or *household* does not always and necessarily intimate the presence of children, if it be admitted that it generally does, it is enough for our purpose. If we have the precedent of the Apostles baptizing households we shall be pretty safe in following their example. There was no need for this purpose that the names, sex and ages of the several members should be given, and unless there be exceptions made, we have no right to make any. It is worthy of remark, that in these instances mentioned there is no notice taken of the profession of any but of the head of the family. Acts xvi. 14, 15. "And a certain woman named Lydia, a seller of purple, of the city of Thyatira, which worshipped God, heard us; whose heart the Lord opened, that she attended unto the things which were spoken of Paul. And when she was baptised and her household, she besought us, saying, If ye have judged me faithful, come into my house and abide there." If it be said that this woman was a single lady and abroad on business, and had no family, we would ask, What was the meaning of her house being baptized? Did Paul dip the building? It is very probable she was a widow; but it is also very certain that she had a family, and that they were baptized, when her heart was opened to receive the things spoken by Paul.

Thus it is evident, that if there had been but this one instance of a household baptism, it would have been probable, that in that house there were children; and that, at any rate, would have been a precedent for baptizing households. It is not, however, solitary. It is recorded, with equal particularity, that, when the jailer believed, he and his were all baptized straightway. v. 38. It was certainly not without design, and so should not be unnoticed, that the two instances of household baptism in this one chapter are one of them under the representation of a female, and the other of a male head. How condescending, gracious, and considerate is our Lord! We have not done yet with instances and evidences of this kind. 1 Cor. 1. 16. "And I baptized also the household of Stephanus." We have then seen three instances of household baptism recorded, without any exceptions made of the children of these professed believers. The mode of recording these transactions evidently agrees with the account of circumcision in Abraham's family. There was no need to give any express statute farther with regard to the privileges of chidren. there was no dispute at that time about this point. The instances of household baptism are doubled and trebled that all doubts might be removed, and all cavils silenced. The first instance would be sufficient for the liberal mind that calculated correctly from ancient usage, and the consistency and grace of God. The second would confirm the more wavering and timid ; the third would, it might be supposed, put the question to rest and stop the mouth of all who would oppose the baptism of the children of the Church. Therefore we conclude that the infants of such as are members of the visible Church, are to be baptized.

If more evidence should be thought necessary, or if more be proper and tolerable after the matter is clear to the candid, we can shew that the Churches, in their ordinary course of religious order, considered the children of professors members, and meet subjects of the holy ordinance of baptism. We have ample evidence to shew the informed and considerate that the custom was uniform, and that instances of household baptism, while they were planting the Church happened frequently. They who are descended of even one professing parent, are called clean and holy. 1 Cor. vii. 14. " For the unbelieving husband is sanctified by the wife, and the unbelieving wife is sanctified by the husband : else were your children unclean ; but now are they holy."

Much depends here upon the meaning you attach to the words holy and clean. Sometimes

O

holy signifies dedicated. All the utensils a-
bout the ancient tabernacle, and temple, were
in this sense holy. The regenerated people of
God, in whom his spirit dwells, are holy. They
are built up a holy temple to be a habitation of
God by the Spirit. It is used more than five hun-
dred times, in scripture, to signify ceremonial purity or meetness for enjoying religious privileges.
This is evidently its signification in this place.
That all the descendants of professors, even when
both parents are credibly pious, are spiritually.
holy, neither Pedobaptists nor Anabaptists will
assert. This inward piety or holiness of heart is
not a thing about which we superficial creatures
are capable of judging correctly, "It is God
that searcheth the heart." In some way howev-
ever, it appears, that the children of one pious
convert were accounted holy. How was this?
Of what external rite or ordinance were they accounted worthy if not of baptism? Can they not
be the subjects of what baptism implies? Cannot the Redeemer, who gathers these lambs in
his arms, and carries them in his bosom, wash
them by his blood? If not, they have assuredly
no part in him. Pious parents will not believe
that their Saviour cannot be the Saviour of their
offspring even in infancy, they will naturally wish,
if at all practicable, to take their children with
them into the Church and kingdom of Christ.
They look with anxiety, whether the arms of
mercy will embrace their babes as a part of themselves. They have found that it does, that al-

though the partner continues yet in unbelief the mercy of the new dispensation is such, that the children are accounted clean and holy, the same as if the unbelieving party had also been sanctified. Yea, in the decision of the Church, he is accounted so far sanctified, even by the believing wife. The meaning which some Anabaptists put upon the word, is quite inadmissable, viz. that it signifies legitimacy of birth. Surely the Apostle would not prove a thing by itself. He would not say, Your marriage is legal and your offspring legitimate because they are so. There is no precedent in the scriptures nor in profane writings for this meaning. There is no instance in the law or usage of any nation, that the christianity or piety of either one or both of the parties, was considered necessary for the legitimacy of the offspring. There was, however, in the usage of the Church, at this time, some difference between the children of professors and those of others. What was it? It must either have been that they were inwardly holy, that the spiritual character of the parents was entailed upon their posterity; or that they were visibly and federally holy and clean.

The former neither Pedobaptists nor Anabaptists will maintain. The latter must therefore be admitted, i. e. such infants, as are descended of parents of whom one or both are credible professors, should be considered clean and holy. They should therefore enjoy all the religious privileges of which they are proper recipients.

Of what outward privileges then could they be the subjects, if not baptism, which is the very first? It need not be urged that according to this reasoning they should also receive the other sacrament. These are very different in their nature. The one is a seal of what infants may participate as well as adults. Surely they may be purged, regenerated, and translated into the kingdom of Christ.

They cannot examine themselves in order to prepare for the other seal. They cannot be edified in the participation of the other sacrament. I can easily conceive of a case, in which an adult might be received to the ordinance of baptism, before he was capable of receiving the proper advantage of the Lord's supper. Birth is necessary for visible existence, and milk is suitable for babes, strong meat must be given only those of full growth, whose minds are exercised to discern good and evil. It seems very evident that there were some of the Corinthian brethren that eat and drank unworthily because they did not discern the Lord's body, who yet were chastened of the Lord that they might not be judged with the world.

We reason then upon this subject conclusively in this manner. We ought to consider all those as members of his Church whom Christ recognizes; but Christ recognises *children* as members of his Church; so should we. Who can exclude those whom Christ the Lord of the house includes? Those children that are, either by birth, or admittance with the parents, members of the Church, should receive the seal and badge of membership ; but baptism is the seal and badge of membership : therefore children should be baptized. The Apostles were commanded to baptize all nations of proselytes, or all those over whom they might afterwards preside, in teaching them to walk in divine institutions. Ministers of the gospel succeed the Apostles, in the discharge of the ordinary negociations of Christ's kingdom. They should, therefore, consider themselves bound to baptize all, whom they could rationally expect afterwards to teach, to observe all things whatsoever Christ commands.

Gospel ministers ought to follow the example of the Apostles in administering divine ordinances ; the Apostles, however, baptised households when the head, or heads, male or female believed ; Therefore, so still should the ministers and stewards of the house and kingdom of Christ baptise the infants of Church members, the households of believers.

What we have reason to believe was a universal and known practice in the Apostolic and primitive Church, we should follow and maintain.

It is well known and must be admitted that in the primitive churches, even of Apostolic planting, the children of professing parents were considered holy ; therefore they should be accounted so still. If we are still urged to give more express commandment, or more obvious example ; we say, let our opponents give more

express commandment, or more obvious example for female right to participate of the Lord's
supper. We say they have a right as well as the
Anabaptist. But we infer it, and so do they.
There is no commandment to dispense it to women; there is no explicit testimony that they
did participate. If then reasoning and inference
be admitted in favour of female rights, why
should they not also be in favor of infants?

Finally, upon the subjects of Christian baptism
and in favor of infants we say, the Christian
Church is the same corporation of the ancient
church called from the subject of it, the Jewish,
not to distinguish it from Christian, but to distinguish it from the Gentile or Catholic Church.
The Church in the wilderness of Arabia, and the
Church in the continent of America is still the
same. The Jewish branches were lopped off the
good olive tree, or ecclesiastical organization, that
we Gentiles might be grafted in. All the rights
and immunities therefore, which they enjoyed, we
should also enjoy. They enjoyed for their children the sign of circumcision, the seal of the
righteousness of which not only Isaac and Jacob
but we also are heirs. Their children were, in
the construction of mercy, held as members of the
church, till they forfeited their right or sold their
birthright. So unquestionably should ours.
Those who were the subjects of the ancient typical rite, should be the subjects of that which came
in its room. Children were the subjects of the
ancient rite or seal, therefore they should of the

modern. Any of these topics of argumentation should be considered conclusive, and I cannot see how any man will candidly examine them, and conclude against them, taken together in their accumulative and corroborative force.

CHAP. II.

The Mode of Christian Baptism.

LET us now see what is the proper mode of Christian baptism.

Here we think, in the first place, it must be admitted on all hands that the water of baptism is not, by any direct power, efficient of spiritual purgation. Of course, it cannot be a matter of moment what its quantity be, only, that it be as much as may be a symbol of the blood of Christ. Even the Brahmins; who impute so much to lotions in the Ganges, consider that it is the holiness of its quality, and not the largeness of its quantity that gives it all its virtue.

All, therefore, must depend upon the divine appointment. Baptism does not avail to the purifying of the flesh ; but as it is the answer of a good conscience, looking to God for a divine blessing upon a divine institution. It must also be admitted, that in the institution of baptism there is no particular direction given respecting the mode thereof. The disciples are commanded to go and baptize ; in what way the water was to be exhibited, the Saviour said nothing.

The word (*baptize*) is one of very indefinite signification. Had the great head of the Church designed that there should be but one mode, it wou'd have no doubt been expressed so that about the mode there could be no doubt. The translators were aware of these facts and so have not translated the word, only given it an English termination, leaving it the same latitude of signification in our language that it had in the original. It is by some considered a causative verb or word from *bapto*; by some it is reckoned a diminutive. Baptists do not consider it as a causative word, for they actually dip, and do not, I believe, generally cause the person, or any other to perform the rite for them. It must, therefore, be understood as a diminutive. I do not say this is very conclusive. I rest the force of the plea for effusion upon convenience, decency and expressiveness. In a rude state of society and in warm climates, where perhaps the principal attention to cleanliness is bodily ablutions and immersions, there may be no great inconveniency experienced in this operation. When people are inured not only to bodily hardship, but when their minds also are destitute of any delicate cultivation, there may, in such a state of society, be no sacrifice of bodily or mental feeling. In such a state of society, the sexes are accustomed to see each other in habits and attitudes, which civil society would count rather awkward. This they may do without either painful or licentious feelings. But in the highly cultivated state of American and British society, certainly every unbiassed mind must feel shocked at seeing the sturdy baptist drag the delicate female into the stream—seize her by the neck and breast, while he trips up her heels in the presence of the gazing crowd. It must require strong feelings of conscience or superstition to reconcile a mind of ordinary delicacy to this mode. If, however, it be commanded, it must be done. We must, in all cases of duty, take up our cross. There is no necessity, however, of making one, and I do not know that in any instance, it is appointed that the members or ministers of Christs flock are to impose these upon each other. They fulfil the law of Christ by bearing one another's burdens. They imitate the corrupt Scribes and Pharisees when they impose onerous loads on Christ's redeemed. It is true offences must come, but woe to them by whom they come. It were, better that a man were cast into the midst of the sea with a millstone at his neck, than that he should offend one of Christ's little ones. . When the wicked of the world treat them rudely because of their testimony in behalf of truth, they must, after the example of their divine Master, hold fast, nor love their lives unto the death for his sake. But does this prove that they must put stumbling blocks and rocks of offence in each other's way—that they will be doing God service when they put one another to death indiscreetly if not intentionally? The Baptist, however, will say all this avails nothing in the face of scripture

authority which is all in favour of dipping.
What is there then in favour of immersion as the
exclusive mode of Christian baptism ? If the
scripture be obviously on that side, then let the
reasoning perish that is opposed to revelation.
Let every imagination be brought into the obedience of faith. The Baptist pleads for immersion, 1 On the precise signification of the word.
2. On the practice of John. 3 On the case of
Philip and the eunuch. 4. On the phrase, "Buried with him by baptism into death." Upon
the first of these arguments we would remark,
Does the word baptize in the English or baptizo
in the Greek signify to dip and nothing else?
If it does not, there can be nothing certainly
learned from the word. If it does, what was the
use of making this word, seeing it and its parent,
according to baptists mean the same thing:

If baptizo and bapto, baptize and dip signify
one and the same thing, why are they not inter-
changeably used? Try an instance in Matthew
iii. 11. " I indeed baptize you with water to repentance ; but he that cometh after me, is migh-
tier than I, whose shoes I am unworthy to bear,
he shall baptize you with the Holy Ghost, and
with fire." Make the word baptize signify nothing but dip, and you may render the passage
thus—I indeed dip you with water, but one cometh after me, &c. he shall dip you with the Holy
Ghost and with fire. Even a baptist, we presume, perceives the solecism and feels shocked
with both the sound and the sense that his own

criticism on the meaning of the word makes.
Will they then say that the word baptize always
means to dip or immerse, and may always be so
translated ? The Jews, it is known, had a great
many washings, sprinklings, and ceremonial purifications, all of which went by the general name
of baptisms. Mark vii. 4. Heb. ix. 10. "And.
when they come from market, except they, wash.
[are baptized, in the Greek];they eat not. And
many other things there be which they have received to hold, as the washing [baptisms] of cups
and pots, brazen vessels-and tables or couches.
Now, it is evident, if they dipped in all their ritual purifications, they must have had very large
ewers or vessels. It will be of importance to
know something about the size of them. As the
shrewd youth remarked, when the very ingenious
and rational preacher taught the people that the
loaves which fed so many thousands were as large
as a certain mountain which he named, "I would
not wish," said the arch wag " to doubt the truth
of what the minister says, but I would like to
know how large the oven was in which the loaves
were baked." If then the Jews baptized brass
kettles, tables, &c. let us examine how large the
vessels were; in which these ritual purifications
were performed. Of these, we have an account
in the anecdote of the marriage at Cana of Gali-
lee. John 11. This family, we have reason to
believe, were as well provided as others and especially at this time. v. 6. "And there were set
six water pots of stone, after the Jews' manner of

purification." How much then did these vessels
contain? Our translation says two or three fir-
kins; in the original, it is two or three measures.
It would have been as well to have left it as indefinite in the translation as in the original, and
if they had put a precise modern measure upon it
they surely ought not to have made such a large
measure as the firkin answer to the original.
The bath has by learned men been thought the
more probable known measure of the *metretas.*
However, some make the bath seven gallons and
a half, some four and some three. The truth is,
it must be more from circumstances than from a
definite knowledge of the word, that we must as-
certain the quantity. However, should these
stone pots contain the largest quantity that any
body ever conjectured, it is evident they could
not admit of a man's body to be immersed in
them. It appears, indeed, from the whole story
to me very evident that they did not contain
more than two or three gallons each. It appears
they were quite handy and portable not only
when they were empty, but also after they were
filled with the wine made of the water. It must
be, therefore, very evident that the baptism performed in these vessels, or vessels of their size,
either of tables or persons must have been a baptism by washing and not by dipping. We know
also beyond any conjecture that the purifications
under the law were performed by sprinklings and
not by immersion. Take for instance the rite of
cleansing the leper. Lev. xiv. And he shall

sprinkle upon him that is to be cleansed from the leprosy seven times and shall pronounce him clean." So also of the unclean house. verses 48, 49, 50, 51, 52. Now, although in both of these cases water was to be afterwards used, it is evident that the typical rite was sprinkling.

By attending to a colloquy in the third chapter of this same book, we will see that baptism was performed by John and the disciples of Jesus in a way, which resembled the rite of purification among the Jews. v. 25. " Then there arose a question between one of John's disciples and the Jews about purifying. v. 26. And they came unto John and said unto him, Rabbi, he that was with thee beyond Jordan, to whom thou bearest witness, behold the same baptizeth, and all men come unto him." Our translators seem evidently to have taken up the proper signification of baptism as used in the New, and also in the Old Testament. It is the same, by which the assembly of divines at Westminster define it, viz. " The washing with water, and as a religious rite having a respect to the great economy of salvation, it must be done in the name of the Father, Son, and Holy Ghost, who in that work take each a proper part." That the translators understood it so and right too, is evident from Heb. ix. 10. " Which stood only in meats and drinks and divers washings [Greek, *baptismous.*] It is here clear to every unprejudiced mind that if they had translated the word baptismous, dippings, as they have done it washings, they would
P

have said a falsehood, from what we have already
seen concerning the legal purifications ; it would
have been improper to have called them dippings,
It was very proper, however, to call them baptisms ; therefore, baptism and dipping are different things. Washing then, it appears, is the radi-
cal idea. From Mark vii. 34 and Luke xi. 38,
it is clear that washing and baptism mean the
same thing. Except they are baptized as it is in
the original, they eat not. What was this baptism ? Why just washing their hands, and what
too is worthy of remark, it was then a custom and
is to this day in the east, to have water poured
on the hands, but no matter how, to be baptized
in the passages cited, was to have the hands
washed, the vessels which the passages say were
baptized, we have seen were washed. One signification therefore of the word baptize is to
wash. Allowing then the baptist his signification
viz. to dip, we shall have another signification of
the word : this with the one made out before will
make two. Let us see if scripture language will
not afford us another sense. In 1 Cor. x. The
Apostle says the Israelites were all baptized unto Moses in the cloud and in the sea. Here was
a baptizing and neither dipping nor washing.
For we can easily see how they might be sprinkled by the spray of the sea and the drops of the
cloud. No honest, unprejudiced reader, and for
such the scripture is designed, would ever think
from the narrative that there was any dipping in
the case as respected the Israelites. The Egyp-

tians and not the Israelites got the immersion, or were dipped on that memorable occasion. It is only a desperate subterfuge in some Baptists, who say they were covered in the cloud and in the sea. Would a Baptist then say that a man might be receiving baptism, while he was walking upon dry ground, provided there was water on every side of him, and a hazy cloud over him? If so, it will be a valuable discovery for delicate constitutions in cold climates. But no, they would not call it baptism, unless they were all wet with water. No man of common sense would call such a positive dipping. The Apostle, however, declares there was a catholic baptism of all the ransomed tribes. It was not done by immersion, for they were not immersed. It was not done by washing, for they were not washed. Still if we give the Apostle credit for true narrative and correct language, they were baptized. Seeing that was performed upon them neither by washing nor dipping, we conclude it was done by sprinkling. To say, they were baptized by water in a vapoury state above them, and in a fluid state at a distance from them, and that this baptism was dipping, is not only inadmissable but absurd and ridiculous. According to this canon of criticism, men might always be called the subjects of baptism when a cloud of vapour impended and waters stood, or run on each side. Unless then, some fourth way be discovered of administering baptism, we must conclude the baptism of the Israelites in the Red Sea was done by affu-

sion. or sprinkling, This then establishes one
important fact which Baptists have unfairly tried
to deny, and shews, to every candid mind, that
the learned and inspired Apostle considered baptism really and properly administered by *sprinkling*. The Apostles, then we see, not only baptized households, but they also evidently considered the word baptism to have the signification
of sprinkling. They would therefore have considered, that they acted according to the tenor,
spirit and letter of their commission, if they laboured to proselyte to the faith of Jesus nations,
and in token of pardon and purgation through
the merit and efficacy of his blood; would sprinkle
the households and nations converted. Why
should not we? Why should not the Baptists
themselves yield to Apostolic authority, and admit that baptism may be valid without immersion? Allow then, dear brethren, the rod of divine authority to dry up the waters of this controversy—suffer the ransomed of the Lord to
pass from Egyptian darkness and vassalage to
the wilderness of ecclesiastical tutorage and the
Canaan of heavenly rest on dry ground. Let the
cloud of divine testimony drop down influences
of heavenly grace on old and young—Let tears
of penitence and gratitude mingle with the symbols of these gracious favours, and so let controversies of words and modes of initiation cease.

The second objection directs us to precedent
and authority.

Here it is to be remarked, in the first place,

that, even if it did appear that John dipped his disciples, I do not know that this would prove dipping to be the only proper way of administering the ordinance of baptism.

1. Because it is not very certain that John's baptism, and that which is appointed in the Christian dispensation, are the same. It is certain it was not instituted by Christ's commandment to his disciples, and through them to the ambassadors of his kingdom. It seems, indeed, rather to have been a baptism in expression of the faith that the kingdom was at hand, than an introduction into the kingdom upon the New Testament plan modelled.

John was not in the kingdom thus modelled himself. "The least in the kingdom of heaven is greater than he." His doctrine was not that the kingdom of heaven was come, but that the kingdom of heaven, or eminent reign of grace in the dispensation of the gospel after Christ's death and resurrection, was at hand. His baptism, therefore, was the baptism of repentance and remission of sins, and reformation of life in expectation of these purer times and stricter dispensation approaching. Thus you see, he was the harbinger of Christ's advent, and not a messenger or minister of Christ, as having already established his Church upon its New Testament and permanent model.

Again—if John did baptize by immersion, and should it be admitted that John's baptism was essentially the same as ours, it does not therefore necessarily follow that we should. There is no necessity, as far as I know, that we should wear a garment of camel's hair girded with a leathern belt, or that our meat should be locusts and wild honey. Unless, therefore, it be made appear, that there is something particularly expressive in this mode ; or that it has positive institution in its favour, we would not be bound, as far as I see, to imitate the minutiæ of John's example.

We have already seen, it has not the latter authority, viz. positive institution, for the commandment was, Go and baptize, not specifying in what mode. Not the former, if the scripture be sustained as a competent judge in the matter ; for the scripture frequently expresses the thing signified in baptism by sprinkling, which is, as we have seen, one of its meanings, but never once, as far as we know, by dipping.

The Israelites varied their mode of eating the passover, and yet neither John nor the Saviour, who were both candid reprovers and strict reformers, found any fault with them on that account. At first, they eat standing upon their feet, with staves in their hands. In Christ's time they eat it in a recumbent posture, after the mode of the Romans in feasting. Christians do not consider themselves bound to imitate all the circumstantial forms of the first eucharistic feast. For instance they do not think it necessary, that this feast should be celebrated in an upper chamber, nor in the night season. It is true, they will reckon themselves bound conscientiously to observe all significant parts of this and every other divine institution. They will, therefore, *take*, in token of the assumption of our nature by our Saviour, which is the great mystery of godliness. They will *break*, in symbol of his suffering for our sins ; *give*, to keep up the sensible remembrance of his free offer of himself for our salvation ; communicants will *receive* as an act of faith appropriating Christ ; *eat*, to shew the hunger of the soul and the satisfying nourishment which is found in the Saviour, who is the true bread of life. They will not consider it a matter of importance, whether they take one little bit of bread or ten. I do not know that the Corinthians would have been reproved for making it literally a feast, if they had not kept up invidious distinctions between the rich and the poor, which is obviously at war with all the principles of the gospel. Still I believe the most of Christians now admit that the Apostle's instructions on that occasion, and the whole character and design of the sacrament, require that small portions of bread and wine should be used. Why such zeal then for copious element in the other sacrament? These facts and inductions however, shew that, in order to keep any ordinance pure and entire, it is not necessary to be minute only where there is obvious signification or express institution involved. We have seen that it is not very certain that John's baptism was Christian baptism ; that if it was, and even if he did immerse, that it is not necessary in another state of society and in another climate that we should immerse. Let us examine, however, before we close the reply to this objection, whether it be very evident that John did administer baptism in this manner.

The first account we have of this matter is in Matth. iii. 6. "And were baptized of him in Jordan, confessing their sins." Now the question is upon this part of the evidence. Did he dip them, or did he wash them, or did he sprinkle them ? All these significations, we have found according to scripture usage, belong to the word. If he dipped them, and the record of the fact was intended to teach us that this mode is essential to the validity of the ordinance, why was it not mentioned in such language, and in connection with such circumstances, (for instance, the changing of apparel) as would have put the matter beyond a doubt ? What renders the assumption of our opponents still more doubtful, is the expression which follows, v. 11. "I indeed baptize you *with* water unto repentance." Now is it not evident that water is here represented as the instrument of baptism, or that with which he performed the ceremony ? But it is also evident that in dipping they do nothing with the water ; they do all with the subject. The water stands or runs. The baptized operates as much upon the water as the baptizer. Try how it will read in the way the dipper would construe it, or with the help of his criticism. You must, of course, use the word in the sense which he says is its proper and exclusive signification. He dipped them with water ; or I dip you with water. That is evidently a solecism or misapplication of terms. I baptize you with water, however makes very good sense. Whether then should we under-stand the word in the way that will make sense or in the way that will act? Our opponents will, perhaps wish to make another emendation of the text, and say that it should be read not that he dipped them with water, which would be inco-herent language, but that he dipped them *in* wa-ter. Allow the alteration and apply the criti-cism to another expression of the same evangel-ist, and in the same chapter. v. 11. " I indeed baptize you with water unto repentance.—He shall baptize you with the Holy Ghost and fire." The same event is predicted in Acts I. 5. " John baptized with water, ye shall be baptized with the Holy Ghost not many days hence." Who-ever will be at the pains of reading and compar-ing these passages either in the original or in our translation; must, if candid, admit that *with*, and not *in*, is the preposition which should be used before water and before the Holy Ghost.

What sense would it make to say, He shall be dipped in the Holy Ghost and in fire, or ye shall be dipped in, &c. It is true there is no prepo-sition at all used before fire, and therefore it might be said in relation to it, that we might ren-der it in that way which would make the best sense. There are two things here which should be noticed. The first is, that the same significa-tion should be attached to an indefinite preposi-

tion expressed as must be attached to the word
without the preposition ; otherwise, there will be
no connection.   It would not do clearly to say,
He shall dip you in the Holy Ghost and with fire.
In the second place, If the syntax of the Greek
language and the scope of the place would require that *puri* without a preposition should be
read with fire as denoting the instrument of purification and not the place in which, then it must
also be evident, that *udati* standing in the same
connection and case, should be in the same way
translated.   Let any man then, at all acquainted
with the Greek, look at the passages cited, and
he will at once see that in this way, the meaning
of the preposition in this place must be *with*, as
denoting the instrumentality of the substance to
which it is prefixed.   But if this be obscure to
some who are unacquainted with biblical criticism, let them but attend to the fact, viz. that
when the prediction was fulfilled, it was not by
immersion, but by affusion.   The disciples were
baptized with the Holy Ghost and with fire on
the day of Pentecost. How was this done ?
Were they dipped in the Holy Ghost ?—dipped
in fire ?   No, the inspired Apostle declares clo-
ven tongues like as of fire sat upon each of them,
and moreover declares that now was accomplish-
ed the ancient prophecy, " I will *pour* out of my
spirit upon all flesh.   Therefore, being by the
right hand of God exalted, and having received
of the Father the promise of the Holy Ghost, he
hath *shed forth this*, which ye now see and hear.

'Thus you see, by comparing one part of the history of John's baptism with another, and all the parts of it with the antitype or that which it prefigured, it is pretty evident that dipping, or immersion was not the mode of its administration. But what renders it still more improbable that they were baptized by dipping is this, "They were baptized, confessing their sins." John seems to have been teaching them, and they confessing, while the ordinance was administered. Now we know when a man dips he has his hands pretty full of business without teaching, and the subjects have other employment for their lips than to confess their sins. This circumstance then upon record, renders it very improbable that he dipped them. If they went down into the water and kneeled, or stooped while he laved or sprinkled water upon them, the instruction and confession might be coetaneous with their baptism, not so if they were thrust under the water or immersed.

We have another text in this chapter, which is frequently cited, or suborned as a witness in this controversy. v. 16. "And Jesus when he was baptized went up straightway out of the water," &c. The shortest reflection will shew you that there is nothing conclusive to be inferred from these words: Nothing but the positive manner in which they have been quoted, could make any person think there was any proof for dipping in the words.

Every body knows that waters, or rivers have

banks, that when you approach the water, even should you only descend or go down to the verge of the river, you may be said to go down into the water; when you recede you may be said to come up from or out of the water, although you have not been plunged all over in or under the water. In corroboration of this construction, we must remember that the baptism of Christ was not of repentance and confession, as that of others, but was a baptism of righteousness. He was about to enter upon the execution of sarcedotal functions, and so must be inducted according to the forms prescribed in Ex. 40, 12. "And thou shalt bring Aaron and his sons unto the door of the tabernacle of the congregation and wash them with water."

As he would not enter upon his public ministry, until he was thirty years of age, according to the statute, so he would observe, as far as circumstances would admit, the law respecting the mode of induction. "Thus it becometh us," saye he, "to fulfil all righteousness." The manner in which this baptism, or washing of the priests at their instalment was performed, we are told in the 31st and 32d verses: The water was applied to their *hands* and their *feet*.

That the expression "into the water," used in relation to those whom John baptized, and which we design shortly more fully to consider, does not necessarily signify to go under the water, is evident from the frequent use of it, in application to mountains. If going "into the mountain" to

pray prove that the mountain was penetrated for
that purpose, then going " into the water" to be
baptized, proves that they were certainly dipped,
or immersed. Further, that nothing can be finally determined by these prepositions is evident
from this plain fact, that it is as expressly stated
that John did baptize " in the wilderness,"
as that he baptized in the river. Did he then
take and dip them in the sand or rocks of the
wilderness ? If the expression prove this, then
the expression " baptized in Jordan will prove
that he dipped. If you compare the records of
Luke and John, you will at once see that all the
signification we are to attach to the preposition,
is the instrumentality of the material, or the
proximity of the place to which it is prefixed.
Luke uses no preposition at all, and it must be
observed that Luke, of all the Evangelists, writes
the purest Greek. Of John he records that he
said, " I indeed baptize you *with* or by water,
" *udati*" i. e. In baptizing I make use of water,
or I apply water to you in baptism. John, the
evangelist, who mixed more Hebrew idiom with
his Greek, uses the preposition which answers to
the *beth* of the primitive language and signifies
with, by, or in. In two places he speaks of John
the baptist. John 1, 26. " I indeed baptize you
with water." Luke before quoted may be used
to explain in what way we should understand
John's preposition. But John himself shews
that the baptism of his namesake was not always
even near by or at Jordan, although it was always

Q

no doubt with water. That it was not confined to Jordan is clear, for in the 28th verse it is stated that he was baptizing in Bethabara beyond Jordan. Again in John iii. 23, it is said, " And John also was baptizing in Enon near to Salim, because there was much water there, and they came and were baptized." It has often been remarked in books on this controversy and in commentaries, that much water, " *udata polla*" signifies many waters rather than a large collection of waters, such as would be requisite for plunging. The very circumstance that it has been somewhat difficult to find the place where this took place shews clearly that there is no large body of water in Enon near Salim. So far as I have been able to gather from travellers and geographers who have described those countries, it would appear that the original expresses the topography of the place better than the translation ; and that the meaning of the phrase rather is, that there was plenty of water to drink and for affusion, than that there was any copious lake or large river for immersion.

The third objection. The case of Philip and the eunuch is urged by the advocates of immersion as very decisive in their favour.

Let us then consider this evidence attentively. There is one circumstance in the fact which renders the case peculiarly worthy of our attention. The Administrator was a gospel minister, or deacon, and the subject was a Gentile believer : Of course we need expect nothing here but what is quite evangelical. If then it be proved that Philip immersed the eunuch of Ethiopia, it ought to have considerable weight as authority in settling the controversy about the mode of Christian baptism. It must also be observed that there is something peculiar in the case. In ordinary cases, it is plain that the administration of this sacrament should be public, and accompanied with the preaching of the word. "Go ye into all the world and preach the gospel to every creature, he that believeth and is baptized shall be saved." We generally expect a plurality of auditors when we preach. Here however, we have the traveller and the preacher without any other human company. The Spirit, however, directed Philip to join himself to this chariot. It is not very likely that they had any convenience of baptising except by approaching some water.

There is another thing also here to be observed; that it is a dry desert where they were travelling between Jerusalem and Gaza. It appears that this prime minister and master of the treasury for Candace, queen of the Ethiopians, was a proselyte of the Jewish religion. It is likely that he had been up at Jerusalem upon some religious business, attending perhaps some of the periodical festivities. The agitated state of Jewish affairs might very probably affect his mind and produce concern. At any rate, he was deeply exercised in his mind, while he read and studied the scriptures. The passage of holy writ, which particularly engaged his attention, was the 3d chap-

ter of Isaiah, and about it he was extremely anxious to know, whether the prophet spake of himself, or of some other man. A mere knowledge
of grammar could not decide his question, for;,
although it was all in the third person, " He was;
led as a lamb to the slaughter, and as a sheep before her shearers is dumb, so he opened not his
mouth." Yet, so common was it, for men who
wrote commentaries and histories, to speak of
themselves, in the third person, that this alone
could not settle the difficulty. Philip, however,
in an opportune season arrived, and preached to
him Jesus the Lamb of God that taketh away the
sin of the world. The eunuch with enlightened
eyes saw the truth of the passage and its fulfilment in the remarkable events of recent occur-
rence. He believed. While they travelled with
minds strongly attent on such a mighty and interesting subject, they came to a certain water, that
seems to have run across the road. This sugges-
ted, at once, to the eunuch, the propriety of having his body sealed with the rite of baptism.
Very probably he would be the more solicitous
for this, because in the same connection and but a
little before the verses he was reading when
Philip joined his chariot, it is said of the same
character on whom his faith was now fixed, "He
shall sprinkle many nations ; the kings shall shut
their mouths at him, for that which had not been
told them shall they see, and that which they had
not heard shall they consider." He was a great
man in the court of Candace, felt himself the sub-

ject of part of this story, and desired to share also of the rest. He had seen and considered
great things which were before hid. When he
saw the water, then he asked Philip, What doth
hinder me to be baptised ? And Philip said, if
thou believest with all thine heart thou mayest.
And he answered and said, I believe that Jesus
Christ is the Son of God. Let the reader keep
all these circumstances in his mind and ask,
What is it in the passage that proves immersion ?
The Anabaptist will say, He went into the water. Well, does this prove that he went under
the water ? If it does, then it is said, as expressively, that Philip went into the water, i. e. as the
Anabaptist explains the phrase, under the water.
" And they went down both of them into the water [under the water, according to the Baptist
comment] both Philip and the eunuch, and he
baptized him." Now let the reader-ask the
plunger, How did Philip baptize the eunuch,
when they were both under the water, before the
rite of baptism was performed ? It will here obviously appear that the passage proves rather too
much for the Anabaptist, upon his own plan of
construing it. Our opponents will be now ready
to say, that common sense teaches that there was
no necessity of Philip's going under the water.
So we think also ; but it is upon the meaning of
words and verbal criticism that we are now reasoning, and if the proof of the eunuch's immersion be good upon the phrase went into the water
and come up out of the water, it must also be good

upon the part of Philip. So the Baptists in order
to be consistent with their own criticism must
accompany their proselytes under the water, and
administer the ordinance the best way they can
in the regions of the deep.

However, we do not wish to insist longer upon
verbal criticism. If he renounces that plea and appeals to common sense, I have no objections provided it be not the common sense of party prejudice. Common sense too, must judge upon facts,
and must remember that baptism is different from
going into the water according to the scripture,
must remember that there is no mention made of
a bridge or a ferry to cross this water, that the
place is a dry desert between Jerusalem and
Gaza, where there is no lake nor river, but that
they came to a certain water ; that there is no
mention made of changing garments, but that as
soon as the simple and easy gospel rite was administered, the Spirit carried away the baptizer,
and the baptized went on his way rejoicing.
Now, I confess, if unprejudiced common sense
say, there is here clear evidence of immersion,
rather than of any other way of baptizing, I cannot see it.

It must also appear evident, that if any portion
of scripture can be found, which will favour the
method of immersion in Christian baptism, it
must be this. The Baptists themselves insist so
much upon it as to shew that they think so too,
and it is evident that if you take their own comment, it will prove too much even for them. If

you reason upon all the circumstances of the narrative, if it be not demonstrably evident, that sprinkling was the mode, it is far more probable that it was sprinkling than immersion.

The 4th objection is taken from Col. ii. 12.

It is evident from this passage that baptism is come in the room of circumcision. All the Churches, as might naturally be expected, were harrassed at that time with Judaizing teachers. These were incapable of resisting the external evidence of the gospel facts, and yet were also incapable of perceiving the spiritual signification of gospel rites. They were envious of Apostolic popularity, and afraid of Jewish or Gentile persecution. In order, then, to reconcile their convictions and policy, their views and ways, they taught a kind of corrupt system, and blended Jewish and Christian rites; they preached the gospel through envy, and, through pride or fear of persecution, taught Christians that they must be circumcised and keep the law of Moses.

The Apostle teaches the Colossians that there was no need of receiving circumcision; for, in so doing, they became debtors to the whole ritual law. He shews them particularly here that they were circumcised virtually, and really by being baptized. They had no need to complain that they were destitute of right rules, or suitable religious rites. All that was moral or spiritual in ancient prescription is certainly retained. For says he " Ye are complete in him who is the head of all principality and power. In whom also ye are circumcised with the circumcision not made with hands, in putting off the body of the sins of the flesh by the circumcision of Christ." The next verse is connected with the one now cited, and shews how all this takes place. v. 12. "Buried with him in baptism, wherein also ye are risen with him through the faith of the operation of God, who hath raised him from the dead."

Is this, then, the closing proof for immersion? If it be, we must see wherein its great strength lieth. There is the more necessity for this, because, we presume that a great many have derived edification from the passage. and yet have never seen any thing in it relating to the mode of administering the ordinance of baptism. However, if it contain evidence and proof relative to this point let us see and own it though it should be rather occult and obscure.

Is this then the argument? Those that are buried are covered with earth ; therefore those that are baptized should be covered with water ? When we are following analogy so close it would be well enough to ask, Whether the dead clothes and coffin do not hinder their entire immersion in the earth ? If that is considered to make no odds in the case of interment, we would again ask, If this might not suggest an improvement upon the Baptist plan of immersion? If the subject were enclosed in a tight box, and box and proselyte deposited in a hole dug in the earth; water might be shovelled upon the box till it was

covered, and the baptized's clothes kept dry.
In this way the common mode of sepulture might
certainly be more completely represented than by
the present mode of immersion. It would certainly, however, be advisable, if such a plan should
be adopted, that the box should be a little farcical
in its size, so as to contain some vital air-lest the
farce should terminate in serious reality as often
as it now does. But we have gone perhaps too
far in shewing how ridiculous this mode of inter-
preting the passage is. Let us see if the plain
and obvious sense of it be not better, viz: That
we die completely to all hopes of life and salvation by the soul-humbling exhibition of the crucified, dead and buried Saviour.

Again—we rise to a newness of life and comfort by the faith of his resurrection. This comm-
ment is confirmed by collation with a parallel
passage in Rom. vi. 3, 4. " Know ye not that so
many of us as were baptized into Jesus Christ,
were baptized into his death ? Therefore we
are buried with him by baptism into death ; that,
like as Christ was raised up from the dead by
the glory of the Father, even so we also should
walk in newness of life." It is certainly proper
that we should understand one scripture by another and one part of the same passage by another. According to this mode of comment it is evident that the rising, in these texts is not a rising
out of the water of immersion, but out of the
grave of a natural state, to walk, not on the banks
of the river, out of which they have ascended, but
to walk in newness of life.

If it should still be urged, that though these expressions do not positively prove that dipping is the only proper plan, they prove that 'it is the more expressive mode of exhibiting those spiritual truths and experience which baptism is designed to represent. 'If that itself were the case, certainly the consideration should have weight. But first, it is certain that Christ, in his baptism unto death was sprinkled. If, in all verbal and ritual institutions, then, we should have respect to Christ and him crucified, to have his death set before us, sprinkling is the best mode. Second. According to both ancient and modern modes of interment, burial is more naturally expressed by sprinkling, than by immersion. We do not plunge the corpse into the earth, but we lay it down and sprinkle mould upon it. We have already seen, that the scripture very often represents the spiritual signification of baptism by sprinkling, but never by immersion. The sum therefore of the matter seems to be this: Baptism has several significations in scripture use; the rite of course may be done in several ways. Ministers are not particularly instructed how they should administer it. Examples from scripture, so far from fixing its meaning to dipping, rather render it incredible, that this was the ancient mode. The most *convenient,* and *decent* way, allowing common sense to judge, is sprinkling, and the most *significant* mode, by the decision of the scriptures is sprinkling. Lev. xiv. 7. Psalm ii. Isa. lii. 15, Ez. xxxvi. 25. Heb. ix. 13, x. 22, xii. 24. 1 Pet. 1, 2.

PART V.

———— ✳ ————

AN ADDRESS TO ANABAPTISTS.

I HOPE, to such of you, as are candid en-quirers for truth and instituted order, this publication will give no offence.

I am the more encouraged to hope this, because it is your ordinary argument and plea, that this sacrament should be administered strictly, punctually, and formally, according to the divine will. You also admit that the divine will is to be learned from the divine word All these are features of professional character, which I can unhesitatingly say, are to me amiable and attractive.

I have thought of you as the Apostle did of his beloved countrymen, that you have a zeal of God, but not according to knowledge. If the matter of fact were as you suppose, if you had all scripture authority upon your side, you would deserve credit for your zeal, tenacity and industry. If the fact be otherwise, you stand in a delicate situation. The decision, upon your side of this controversy, is a very responsible one.

You decide not only that infants are not, cannot be members of the Church of Christ, but you decide also that the great body of Christian professors are unbaptized, and that the great majority of Christian ministers are unordained. You ought really to pause, and maturely weigh arguments upon both sides, before you decide and act upon such heavy matters. This certainly ought not to be done, by, "So I think ; or so brother or elder such a one thinks. The Father of the Spirits of all flesh must decide this ; the Redeemer of the Church who purchased her with his own blood, and who will finally judge every one according to his works, must settle this, and every other controversy. But his will is to be known from his word. Let that supreme standard then be candidly examined and fairly interpreted. You must not examine the sacred word with the spirit of party ; but in candour and with the spirit of God. Compare the passages generally cited on this controversy with one another, and with the scope and tenor of the parts wherein they are found, and with the word generally. Examine them in the light of divine grace. Remember as you read, This book is a history of redeeming love and divine grace. With regard to plain matters of fact we would have you to consider, that the examples of adult baptism recorded in the scriptures do not authorize you to re-baptize. Those who are mentioned as having been subjects of adult baptism, you must remember, were not baptized in infancy or youth. Now, if it be found that you are judging another

man's servants in a matter, which they perform
upon as sound principles, and with as much faithfulness as you, it will not leave you in a comfortable situation.   Have you no fears that you,
thereby, take the name of God in vain by repeat-
ing that ordinance, which ought on one subject
to be but once exhibited?   We demand of you
before you do this any more to produce authority.
Before the sixth, or even before the sixteenth
century, where is there any instance of adult baptism, upon the principle that infant baptism was
invalid and improper?   There were some whose
parents had been negligent. Some whose parents died, and no satisfactory sponsor being found
it was thought best in some cases to delay their
baptism. Some deferred the reception of this
ordinance upon the same principle that communion is now delayed, viz. upon superstitious fears
and licentious propensities ; some put off this
ordinance until they would reach their thirtieth
year; some till they could be baptized in Jordan; and some till they could have it administered
by a favorite bishop. There were some, such as
the Waldenses and Albigenses, who had not a
good opportunity of having this ordinance time-
ously and purely dispensed. They plead that it
was not essential to salvation ; they would rather have it undone than done by the corrupt
Church of Rome. But where is the instance of
their baptizing any of those who joined them
even from that very corrupt Church ?   And even
if they had, this would no more be an evidence
R

that they denied infant baptism, than instances of
re-baptism among the Donatists and Novatians
would be a proof that they denied what they practised. They baptized proselytes from other con-
nections, because they denied their authority altogether, and not because they denied infant
baptism. The Waldenses, however, we believe,
generally took the view of this matter which the
subsequent Reformers have, and distinguished
between the validity of an ordinance and the purity of its administration; sustaining the former in
many cases where they could not admit the latter. Thus the Waldenses testified against the
Popish notion, that baptism was regeneration or
essential to salvation. They testified against the
superstitious appendages which Papists had af-
fixed to this simple, but very expressive ordinance. But that they did not deny the validity
of infant-baptism, is evident from two notorious
facts.

First. When the Reformers and they united,
they never required the Reformers to be re-baptized, nor the ministers of them to be re-ordained.
All the objection they had to the denomination,
Reformed, was, that it seemed to imply that those
so named had apostatized which they had not.

Second. The Reformers always speak very
favourably of the Waldenses, and always speak
very bitterly against the factious and heretical
Anabaptists. That they called and accounted
them heretical and disorderly did not make them
so, but that they spoke of them, in such terms,

while they were following the steps, and approving
of the measures of the Waldenses, proves plainly
that the Waldenses and the Anabaptists were
then considered very different characters. I will
also admit too that a number of the Anabaptists
have by experience acquired more prudence than
those who first disgraced with their errors, and
disturbed with their factions, the cause of Protestants. Still, you must not take it amiss, if Pœ-
dobaptists, who can give you authority for their
practice from the first and second century down,
ask you, from whom have you derived your origin? It is clear that according to your system
such an account is very necessary, much more so
than with others, who, while they are as tenacious
of truth and order, are more liberal in making al-
lowances, and more learned, as I would say, in
making judicious distinctions. What will become of you, if it ieally appear that you have neither John the Baptist nor the Apostles, the
primitive churches, the Waldenses, nor the Reformers as your predecessors and patrons? You
deny our ordinances, our ecclesiastical authority.
Who first dipped the baptist brother? Who first
ordained the baptist elder? You ought to know
this very correctly, lest it be found that your own
system and mode of judging will judge and condemn yourselves. Here you must not misunderstand me; I am not judging you, but expos-
ing you to judge yourselves. Take your present
practice as the rule of your decision. If you
find that it is going to leave you fatherless, spu-

rious and self created, we hope it will teach you
to judge of others more charitably. Still, however, I would not have you think that I am urging you to the loose practice of the Church of
England, which allows for secular purposes every
profane creature, and people of every creed to
partake of the holy communion. No, if you
think us "disorderly brethren," treat us as such;
"withdraw from us," till you be convinced of the
contrary. But do not excommunicate us altogether from the visible church, because we have
not been baptized at the particular time, and in
the precise mode which you think proper.

We will readily admit that not only the Popish
harlot, but also many Protestant societies have
turned the Church too much into a worldly sanctuary, have admitted many both old and young
to membership, neither for their own good nor for
the honour of the Church, which should be a
holy society. But is it fair, on that account, to
infer that God hath cast off his people and their
seed? Surely some of you have a sense of the
great grace of God in Christ. Let such consider
that "He gathers the lambs in his arms, and carries them in his bosom." Ought not then his
ministers to feel their obligation, if they have
tasted that the Lord is gracious, to feed his
lambs? If they have ever got a gracious and re-
claiming look from Jesus whereby they say we
love him, because he first loved us, they *must*
feel this obligation; if they do, are they to prepare for them as of the household of faith, or as

belonging to the world ?   If in the former sense,
why do you not act consistently, and recognize
their membership in the family of Jesus !   If in
the latter, you put the children of believers in a
strange predicament.   They visibly belong to the
world, and yet their parents belong to the church.
See how you divide families, and this too before
they can divide themselves.   See how contrary
to the principles of all civil society, the grace of
God, and the pious wish of every godly parent
you act.

But you will say, We consider the children of
parents that are pious as possessing great privileges, and the parents themselves as under great
obligations to bring up their children in the nurture and admonition of the Lord.   Here again
by considering the good of the child you impose
a hard task upon the parent.   You urge him to
have constantly to do without those that are visibly without.   You urge the parents to work without straw, to labor without symbol or promise.
If, moreover, the religious education of children
be a duty, why should we not vow to do that duty
as well as others ?   " Vow and pay to the Lord
your God."   If we cannot succeed in bringing
them up for God, we shall be clear of our oath
like Abraham's servant.   But certainly we have
very comfortable promises and it does seem to
me very improper, very imprudent, very unbelieving and very ungrateful not to apprehend
them.   " Train up a child in the way he should
go, and when he is old he will not depart from it."

You still ask, What is the use of this ordinance? I answer it has six uses. First, It is a
recognition of the grace of God. Second, It is a
gratification of the pious parent. Third, It is a
rendering to God what is his due. Fourth, It is
a religious bond of mutual duties among godly
families. Fifth, It is a solemn pledge of the permanency of the Church, and a bond among the
several members thereof. Sixth, It is calculated
in a peculiar manner to establish the mind of a
pious parent, either when he is about to leave his
offspring or when they are called away from him.
In the acknowledgement of divine grace and mercy, justice ought not to be denied. In the baptism of infants the fall of man, in Adam is acknowledged. That this affects infants is obvious,
in the dispensations of Providence, why should not
the covenant and dispensation of grace also affect
this interesting class of juniors? You see their
faces often bedewed with sorrow and sometimes
pale with death, why will you not allow true believers to have their children's faces sprinkled
with the symbol of the grace of life? Why not
allow us to acknowledge the grace of God, who
" forasmuch as the children were partakers of
flesh and blood, did himself also take part of the
same, that through death he might destroy death"
&c. Our elder Brother knows what it is to be a
babe as well as to be a man. If babes had not
needed redemption by his blood, why should he
have been circumcised in youth? The promises
are all ratified in him; the testament, in which

they are contained He sealed with his blood..
Are there then any promises to children ?: If none,
where is the great grace of this dispensation ?
The promises were to be to the seed. If the promise be to the children still, why should not the seal
also be ? It is not safe to separate that which.
God hath joined.. It is evident that God has appointed baptism as the sign and pledge of regeneration ; to whom he denies it therefore, he must
be considered as denying the grace signified..
Why is it the will of God that unbelievers and.
impenitent sinners should not be baptized ? It.
is because he denies them the grace, he will not,
grant them the sign. If, therefore, God denies.
the sign to the infant seed of believers, it must-
be because he denies them the grace of it ; and.
then all the children of believing parents dying
in their infancy, must. without- hope perish..
Moreover, I argue, if the promise be not to the
seed of believers, it cannot be to believers themselves. What was the promise? "I will be your
God and the God of your seed." Take away the
latter part of it and it is not the same promise.
Again, Christ came to ratify the promise made
to the fathers, Rom. xv. 8, why then, will you,
not allow us to acknowledge this grace of the
Redeemer? Why not help us to do it ? Surely you would not have him that is the messenger
of the covenant, Mal. iii. 1, to come to disannul
the covenant; if this had been the case, then
Christ had not been a. faithful messenger, and.
those who say that infants have no part in the

promise and the seal, necessarily deny that He came to confirm the promises made unto the Fathers. You will make as little of it to say, that the promise which is to believers and their seed is the promise of the Spirit. Let it be so, that is the same promise. How is God our God but by granting us his Spirit. This is the very blessing which was promised and fulfilled to Abraham in the ancient dispensation of grace, and which is now graciously transferred to us poor Gentiles. Gal. iii. 13. "Christ hath redeemed us from the curse of the law, being made a curse for us : for it is written, Cursed is every one that hangeth on a tree. v. 14. That the blessing of *Abraham might come on the Gentiles through Jesus Christ, that we might receive the promise of the Spirit through faith.*"

Hear what Dr. Owen, who can be charged by none as a superficial man, says upon this passage: " Christ is the messenger of the covenant. Mal. iii. 1. (i. e.) the covenant of God made with Abraham. Gen. xvii. 7. 1. That covenant was with and to Christ mystical. Gal. iii. 16. And he was the messenger of no covenant, but that which was made with himself and his members. 2. He was sent, or was God's messenger to perform and accomplish the covenant and oath made with Abraham. Luke i. 72, 73. 3. The end of his message and of his coming was, that those to whom he was sent, might be blessed with faithful Abraham, or that the blessing of Abraham promised in the covenant might come on them." Gal. iii. 9, 14.

To deny this overthrows the whole relation between the Old Testament and the New ; the veracity of God in his promises, and all the properties of the covenant of Grace mentioned, 2 Sam. xxiii. 5. It was not the covenant of works, neither originally, or essentially, nor the covenant in its legal administration ; for he confirmed and sealed that covenant, of which he was the Messenger ; but these he abolished. Let it be named what covenant he was the messenger of, if not of this. Occasional additions of temporal promises do not in the least alter the nature of the covenant. Herein he was the minister of the circumcision for the truth of God to confirm the promises made to the Fathers. Rom. xv. 7. That is undeniably the covenant made with Abraham, enlarged and explained by the following premises. This covenant was, that God would be a God to Abraham and to his seed, which God explains to be his infant seed. Gen. xvii. 12. that is; the infant seed of every one of his posterity that should lay hold on, and avouch that covenant as Abraham did and not else. This the whole Church did solemnly for themselves, and their posterity whereon the covenant was confirmed and sealed to them all. Exod. xxiv. 7, 8. And every one was bound to do the same in his own person, which if he did not, he was to be cut off from the congregation whereby he forfeited all privileges to himself and his seed.

The covenant therefore was not not granted in its administrations to the carnal seed of Abra-

ham as such; but to his covenant seed, those
who entered into it, and professedly stood to its
terms. And the promise made to the Fathers
were, that their infant seed, their buds and offspring, should have an equal share in the covenant with them. Isa. xxii. 24, xliv. 3. lxi. 9,
lxv. 23. They are the seed of the blessed, and
their *offspring with them*; not only themselves,
who are the believing professing seed of those
who were blessed of the Lord by a participation
of the covenant, Gal. iii. 9. but their offspring also, their buds, their little ones are in the same
covenant with them. If this be not so under the
New Testament—if believers, those who lay hold
on and avouch the covenant of God, be not taken
into covenant with their infant seed, their buds
and offspring; then was not Christ a faithful
messenger, nor did he confirm the truth of the
promises made unto the fathers.

To deny, therefore, that the children of believing, professing parents, who have avouched God's
covenant as the church of Israel did, Ex. xxiv.
7, 8, have the same right and interest with their
parents in the covenant is plainly to deny the fidelity of Christ in the discharge of his office. It
may be it will be said that although children have
a right to the covenant or do belong to it, yet
they have no right to the initial seal of it. This
will not suffice: For, 1: If they have any interest
in it, it is either in its grace or in its administration. If they have the former, they have the
latter also, as shall be produced at any time: If

they have neither, they have none. Then the
truth of the promises of God unto the Fathers,
was not corfirmed by Christ. 2. That to whom
the covenant or promise doth belong, to them be-
longs the administration of the initial seal of it, is
expressly declared by the Apostle. Acts ii. 38,
39, be they who they will? 3. The truth of God's
promise is not confirmed, if the sign and seal of
them be denied ; for that whereon they believed
that God was a God to their seed, as well as to
themselves, was this, that he granted the token
of the covenant to their seed as well as to themselves ; if this be taken away by Christ, then,
faith is overthrown, and the promise itself is not
confirmed ; but weakened as to the virtue it hath
to beget faith and obedience. Wherefore, the
right of the infant seed of believers to baptism,
as the initial seal of the covenant, stands on the
foundation of the faithfulness of Christ, as the
Manager of the covenant, and Minister of God
for the confirmation of the truth of the promises,
and those who deny it, deny the faithfulness of
Christ, though not intentionally, yet by unavoida-
ble consequence." From all this then you may
see one important use of infant baptism. *It is a
public recognition of the never-failing grace of
God.* Second. It is a gratification of pious parents. This use of infant baptism will not be considered a frivolous argument for the continuation
of the practice, if we consider the analogies of
nature, and the special clemency and kindness of
this dispensation of grace. Parental affection,

liberalized by an extensive contemplation of God's ways, encouraged by scriptural precedents and promises, and especially when animated by divine grace, will cry, O that the child might live before thee! Gen. xvii. 18. He who hears the young ravens and the young lions, hears the distress and affliction of young mortals, and will gratify the pious prayers and earnest supplications of parents in their behalf. Behold the distressed Hannah travailing in her soul, before she conceived in her body, praying and weeping and vowing.—Read the instructive and encouraging passage, 1 Sam. 1, 9—18. Was the disconsolate Hannah neglected? No. Was the story recorded only for entertainment? No. With all other scripture it was designed for direction in righteousness. Mark then, ye mothers in Israel, her conduct. She calls him Samuel, that is, asked of God, and she presents him again to the Lord, saying, "He whom I have obtained by petition shall be returned." Her dedication of him is accepted; the pious parent is justified. This particular favour she acknowledges in an inspired hymn. The same general principle in relation to God's kind and condescending disposition is noticed in the thirty-seventh psalm and fourth verse " Delight thyself also in the Lord, and he shall give thee the desires of thine heart."

Can parents help having desires, fond desires for the salvation of their children? Can they be indifferent about obtaining every help of their faith? Can they, then, say that baptism is of no use, when it seals to their offspring the promises of salvation? Christian parents know that God's word is sure, but still the considerate of them will rejoice that he establishes their faith by two immutable things. Party spirit, I admit, may prevail so much, in some, as to deprive them of natural affection; but we are speaking of ordinary cases, and can our Baptist friends suppose that God will reckon their neglect of their children, self denial and humility? No. He will ascribe it, if not to cruelty, to forgetfulness and ignorance. "Even the sea monsters draw out the breast; they give suck to their young ones: the daughter of my people is become cruel, like the ostriches in the wilderness." Lam. iv. 3. See a farther description of this unnatural animal in Job xxxix. 14. "Which leaveth her eggs in the earth, and warmeth them in the dust; 15 and forgetteth that the foot may crush them, or that the wild beast may break them. 16 She is hardened against her young ones, as though they were not her's: her labour is in vain without fear. 17 Because God hath deprived her of wisdom; neither hath he imparted unto her understanding." We would then affectionately exhort those, who have yet some bowels of affection for their children, to take courage, and bring them to the king of Israel, who is a merciful king, although he may suffer you to be greatly exercised in mind about their right (so if you are pious you have been about your own) yet, he delights to gratify your pious solicitude for your offspring,

S

and will approve even what some ill informd disciples may call presumptive audacity. Read for confirmation of this truth Math. xv. 21, 28—Mark vii. 24. You will certainly be more safe in imitating the approved example of the Syrophenician than in following the wild Arabian of the desert. See how even the woman of Canaan entreats for her young daughter, even in the face of frowning disciples, and a remonstrating Jesus, and she succeeds !!! Shall there be less faith among the matrons of Israel, who bring forth children whom the God of Israel claims as his? But this brings us to the *Third Use* of infant baptism, which we have stated, viz. *That it is a rendering unto God what is his due.*

If faith be too feeble to appreciate the force of the first inducement, and calculation on divine kindness too low to catch the strength of the second, we would fondly hope, that a sense of justice would remove all scruple from the minds of our opponents, about the propriety of Christians dedicating their infant offspring to God in baptism. You listen to constables and collectors when they proclaim in your ears, "Render unto Caesar the things that are Caesar's," and shall you not attend to the legates of heaven, when they call upon you to " Render unto God the things that are God's ?" The very first principle of equity and justice is, to give every one his due. If, therefore, we can shew that the children of believers are his, you will allow him his due. That which is, in a peculiar sense, his, ought in a peculiar way to be

marked as his. The children of his covenant
people are in a peculiar sense his ; therefore, the
children of his covenant people should be in a
peculiar way marked as his property. I have
been the more particular in framing this argument, because, however solid its principle, it is
liable to the attacks of insolent quibble. We
shall not insult your understandings so far as to
tell you, that this principle has the sanction of antiquity and obvious propriety both upon its side;
but we would wish you to attend to two facts,
which render its propriety, *now*, more obvious
than in ancient times. First. In the patriarchal
and Mosaic dispensations, God's people were lo-
cally distinct from others, and so had less need of
being peculiarly marked. Secondly. Society, at
that time was not so formal in its negociations as
latterly it has been. Every shepherd and mer-
chant can appreciate these observations, and apply them to the case in hand. These thoughts
being kept in view, the conduct of those who profess to be under shepherds, and yet oppose the
application of these principles to the lambs of
Christ's flock, must appear to the candid very
suspicious. Forget, I entreat you, dear friends,
that you are baptists, and think, should not those
who love Christ pay marked attention to *his
lambs ?* Listen to what David or Solomon says,
" Lo, children are an heritage of the Lord ; and
the fruit of the womb is his reward."* To every pious parent, the Lord, whose heritage chil-

* Psalm cxxvii. 3.

dren are, says, "*Take this child, and nurse it for me.*"† "Thus saith the Holy One of Israel, and his maker, Ask me of things to come concerning *my sons*, and concerning the works of my hands, command ye me.' § Shall Christian worshippers, of the true God suffer idolators to be more entire-ly devoted to their imaginary deities, and be more honest in their dealings with lying vanities, than they are in their transaction with the Blessed and, only Potentate, King of kings and Lord of lords? Ezek. xvi. 20, 21. "Moreover, thou hast taken thy sons and thy daughters, whom thou hast born unto me, and these hast thou sacrificed unto them to be devoured. Is this of thy whore-doms a small matter? 21 That thou hast slain my children, and delivered them to cause them to pass through the fire for them?" The children of idolators are reckoned the children of the idol. Mal. ii. 11. "Judah hath dealt treacherously, and an abomination is committed in Israel and in Jerusalem; for Judah hath profaned the holiness of the Lord which he loved and hath *married the daughter of a strange god.*"

We admit that adult believers are not unfre-quently called children of God. Math. v. 9. "Blessed are the peace makers for they shall be called the children of God." This is so far, how-ever, from militating against the plea of God's pe-culiar propriety in the children of believers, that it seems to me entirely in favour of it. If he had no people that were literally children, we can-

<hr>

† Ex. ii. 9.　§ Isa. xlv. N.

.not see upon what principle he would call some metaphorically so.. He seems to take, if we may so speak, a pleasure in calling his people generally by that name, because of such is the kingdom of God.. We are not to be understood, however as advocating the right of those, who have descended from any distant predecessor, or of those who are adult descendants of an immediate parent who is or was pious: Rom. ix. 7. " Neither because they are the seed of Abraham are they all children, but in Isaac shall thy seed be called. 8. That is, they which are the children of the flesh, these are not the children of God; but the children of the promise are counted for the seed." Here I very readily admit that the Apostle has a reference to a supernatural birth according to a sovereign election, as the scope of the place will prove to every enlightened student; still it is well known that the descendants of the pious patriarch had a peculiar mark of being God's peculiar property, until the seed of the flesh despised the seed of the promise in adult years; and this too without any regard to evidences of regeneration, which could not then be obtained. This is the principle we would have you, in justice to God and your seed, still to observe. Reject not, we pray you the counsel of God against your offspring, in refusing to have them baptized. If, when they grow up, they behave rudely as did Ishmael in Abraham's house, let their baptism become no baptism; let them be ejected. If, like Esau, they sell their birthright

s 2

you cannot help that, but for justice's sake let
babes, while babes, have their birthright. Let
the children of the promise be accounted for the
seed still. In doing so you are certainly making
no great sacrifice. We are not calling upon you
to give them to the arms of a burning Baal or
a monstrous devouring Moloch, but you are giving them to the arms of a merciful Jesus, ac-
knowledging the virtue and value of his redeeming blood to purify souls and purchase captive
children. If you the roots be holy, so are they
the branches, upon every analogy of nature and
gracious dispensation. Ye have had your holiness or consecration to God signified by baptism,
why should not your branches receive the same
ordinance? Will you not allow God by his
Spirit efficiently, and by his ministers symbolical-
ly, to pour his Spirit upon your seed and his blessing upon your offspring?* Will you not allow
the Redeemer of his Church to sanctify and
cleanse all the members thereof, young and old,
with the washing of water by the word?†

Fourth. It is a spiritual and religious bond of
mutual duties among godly individuals and families. All the ordinances of religion, as well as
the arrangements of Providence, are evidently
calculated to bind men together by social ties.
Any usage, therefore, of the Church, which con-
forms to this general principle, is so far demonstrated to be consistent with the great whole.
Any usage, on the contrary, which does not con-

* Isa. xliv. 3. † Eph. v. 26.

form to this great social principle, is so far doubtful. By baptism administered to infants we obtain a solemn bond of parents, that they shall perform parental duties conscientiously to their children. There are few, we believe, so fanatical, as to say 'that parents do not owe some duties to their children, or to God, in relation to their children. There are few willing so far to acknowledge themselves descendants of Cain, as to say they should exercise no brotherly guardianship towards each other in relation to these duties. For the illustration of the practical advantage of infant baptism, in this view of the subject, we shall suppose two cases. 1st. Of two christian brethren who acted upon the plan of infant baptism and parental vows in the administration of *that* ordinance. 2d. Of two belonging to your society, who deny that infants are, or can be, members of the Church, and, of course, have no baptismal vow in immediate relation to their offspring. One of each of these parties has naughty children, and, like Eli, does not, with sufficient energy and faithfulness, restrain them. One of each of these parties is exemplary, in his own conduct, and conscientious and vigilant to inspect reprove and reform his Christian brother. Upon the Pædobaptist system, the correct man can say to the offender, Dear brother, I am truly sorry to find that you so far forget your covenant engagements for your children, that you suffer them to live in ignorance, and in all that train of vice, and dissipation which haunt untutored youth.

Did not you, when presenting your children before the Lord in baptism, vow, under all the solemnities of sacramental symbols there exhibited,
that you would instruct them in the principles,
and train them up in the practices of an holy religion?—that you would not only set before
them a pious example, but also that you would
use towards them a strict discipline, that they
might not be allowed to profane the holy name
whereby they were called, by following the propensities of the flesh, the fascinations of the world
and the standard of the prince of darkness, who
rules over the children of disobedience?

The offender cannot in consistency but say, I
acknowledge your reproof is proper. I have
been too indulgent and too negligent. I have
verily been faulty in the holy covenant; I confess I have not only dishonoured God, but also
have given offence to my ecclesiastical brethren,
who are united with me in the same covenant.
All the comfort, I can now have is, that the God
of Israel is merciful and ready to forgive, that he
promises to heal our backslidings. Were not the
covenant itself sure and steadfast, what would
frail, failing mortals do? Dear brother, help me
by your prayers, advice, and co-operation to reform my family, that we may yet walk together
in the light, as children of the light, rejoicing that
the blood of Jesus Christ, which was sprinkled
sacramentally upon us all in baptism cleanseth us
from all sins. On the opposite system, what
shall the aggrieved say! What cannot the offen-

der reply ? Does the former adduce, from general topics of morality, arguments to convince his brother of the impropriety of his conduct towards his family? By this very fact you may see the imperfection of your system. Why does not your system embody these principles in the social compact? Even should there be some articles in the congregational covenant; relative to family government; it is clear that all sources of purification must be very liable to run dry, which are not connected with the fountain opened in the house of David for sin and for uncleanness. The great argument for, and the great agent of, sanctification in young or old must be, and is, the blood of Christ. Why then weaken that argument, why keep out of view the operation of that agent, in relation to your infants? What would your system answer should the reproved in the case before us say, " What have I to do with those that are without," alluding to his own children? Would the laws of civilized society admit this answer; and is the system of your church less perfect? Suppose the first founders of the Anabaptist society had succeeded in demolishing this fabric of civil government altogether, by what laws would you either have corrected or protected your children? In the same way the advantage of infant baptism might be demonstrated from the hold upon youth which it affords to the ministers of the gospel. The covenant connexion established by circumcision, the Apostles employed as an argument with the Jews in urging them rightly to improve the opportunities of the gospel. Acts iii. 19. "Repent ye therefore, and be converted, that your sins may be blotted out, when the times of refreshing shall come from the presence of the Lord. v. 25. Ye are the children of the prophets, and of the covenant which God made with our fathers, saying unto Abraham; And in thy seed shall all the kindreds of the earth be blessed." Even in their negociations with churches composed of a considerable proportion of Gentiles, they draw arguments from the ancient covenant which embraced the infants and households of professors. Thus, in urging upon the Romans the great duties of forbearance, mutual edification and united profession and reciprocal charities, he says "Wherefore receive ye one another as Christ also received us, to the glory of God. Now I say that Jesus Christ was a minister of the circumcision for the truth of God, to confirm the promises made unto the fathers; and that the Gentiles might glorify God for his mercy; as it is written, For this cause I will confess to thee among the Gentiles and sing unto thy name." Rom. xv. When reproving the Galatians for their legal views and carnal disposition to be made perfect by the flesh, he recommends to them evangelical views, and spiritual exercises by the example of Abraham. Gal. iii. 6. "Even as Abraham believed God and it was accounted to him for righteousness. v. 7. Know ye not that they which are of faith, the same are the children of Abraham?" Children must ex-

pect to be justified upon the same principles of
their parents, Abraham was a very opposite example to those who were proselyted in adult
years, and were made the fathers in a new dispensation. v. 8. "And the scriptures, foreseeing that
God would justify the heathen through faith,
preached *before the gospel* unto Abraham, saying;
In thee shall all nations be blessed. v. 9. So then
they which be of 'faith' are blessed, with faithful
Abraham ;" as if he had said, You are entirely
bewitched and dreadfully deceived, if you suppose
that Abraham was justified by the law, or sanctified by external and ritual ceremony..

It seems from this last quotation obvious that
the Apostle found no difficulty in counteracting
the tendency of Judaizing teachers, inconsistency with maintaining the evangelical principles and
spiritual tendency of the Abrahamic dispensation. Those whom he reproves and their teachers, saw nothing but legal principles and carnal
forms in it; they considered it as a fleshly covenant, by conforming to the bodily exercise of
which, they might obtain salvation. Thus you
see, so far you and these deluded Galatians agree,
and had the Apostle been of the same mind with
them and you on this point, he must evidently
have taken quite other ground to refute them.
But, by the Spirit of truth, he is preserved from
that extreme, and shews, in the form of his reasoning, the advantage of having, in all our ecclesiastical proceedings, some view to a permanent,
general and conspicuous covenant. Without this

Christians will have upon each other no bond, even from the venerable revelation of truth, legislation of divine sovereignty, nor from the successive dispensations of God's grace.

Fifth. It is a solemn pledge of the permanency of the Church ; and of course, in gloomy times, is an exhibition of cheering future prospects.

No truth is plainer than this, that "one generation passeth away, and another cometh." Were the former only true, and nor the latter, all human society must inevitably become extinct. A permanent society, therefore, must have men, women, and *children* for its members. Take away any one of these and it becomes visibly imperfect. If it continue it must for that continuance be dependant. Is the Church, then, an imperfect and a dependant society, in its visible organization and obvious structure ? So say the opponents of infant membership and infant baptism ; but so says not the Bible. The Christian, while he contemplates, with pleasure, the correspondence of the charter and the seal of the covenant with respect to the persons interested in the promises, will also rejoice that the correspondence holds out a sure pledge of the permanency of the Church. We are not reasoning with you now that it does so, or we would be more particular in stating our arguments, but we are shewing that it is not in vain that this is done. It gladdens the hearts of those who love the prosperity of Zion and rejoice in her permanent charter and permament seals. When the good old man feels his infirmities multiply, and is anticipating from year to year, his own dissolution, it will do his heart good to see an infant presented before the Lord in baptism. He will then remember that the Lord hath said, " My mercy will I keep for him for evermore, and my covenant shall stand fast with him. His seed also will I make to endure for ever." Psalm lxxxix. 28. Frail as he is and fleeting as he sees all nature to be, he will rejoice in the permanent establishment of the church and the continuation of her infant members. "The children of thy servant shall continue, and their seed shall be established before thee." cii. 28. Are the children related to him? He will feel as if this promise was immediately fulfilled to himself. "Yea, thou shalt see thy children's children, and peace upon Israel." cxxviii. 6. He will pray that that may be fulfilled to the children. " I will pour my spirit upon thy seed and my blessing upon thy offspring, and they shall spring up as among the grass, and as willows by the water courses." Isa. xliv. 4. He will pray that the substance as well as the sign may be present. Isa. xliv. 4. As for me, this is my covenant with them, saith the Lord, My spirit that is upon thee, and my word which I have put in thy mouth, shall not depart out of thy mouth nor out of the mouth of thy seed, nor out of the mouth of thy seed's seed, saith the Lord from henceforth and for ever." lix. 21. Behold the scene a little produced, see those children join

T

in the cheerful exercises of the sancturary and
tell what, good man, or angel, can but be pleased?
Take but one peep in Zechariah's glass, viii. 3.
"Thus saith the Lord I am returned unto Zion,
and will dwell in the midst of Jerusalem, and Jerusalem shall be called the city of truth ; and the
mountain of the Lord of hosts. There shall yet
old men and old women dwell in the streets of
Jerusalem and every man with his staff in his
hand, for very age. 5. And the streets of the city
shall be full of *boys* and *girls* playing in the streets
thereof." If the prophet gives us a fair representation, a true picture of the Church in her
Millenial glory, you see *children shall be in her
streets.* Who is so misanthropic as to wish it
should be otherwise?

Sixth: It is calculated in a peculiar manner,
to support the mind of a pious parent, either
when he is about to leave his offspring, or when
they are called away from him.

The more religion there is upon any possession the more highly will its enjoyment be relish-
ed, and the more easily will its alienation be
borne. The parent naturally wishes to see his
children comfortably established in the world
and in the Church before he and they separate.
He may, in this, be disappointed. Is he called
away before they grow up ? In baptism he has
already dedicated them to God in a solemn covenant, and in a voluntary and cordial manner.
It will be easy for him, therefore, now to comply
with the scriptural injunction. Jer. xlix. 11,

"Leave thy fatherless children, I will preserve them, and let thy widows trust in me." Are they wrested from him in early infancy, with Job, he says, "the Lord giveth and the Lord taketh away, and blessed be the name of the Lord," or with David in faith of seeing them in the immortal country, he says, "I will go to him, he shall not return to me." Is the good man taken off, while his children are young, but not before he has got evidence that they are going to be active in building up the Church, the temple of the living God? Will he not, in that case, take up David's soliloquy, when Nathan told him that his son should build the intended house, for which he had laid up so much treasure? "Who am I, O Lord God? and what is my house that thou hast brought me hitherto? And this was yet a small thing in thy sight, O Lord God, but thou hast spoken of thy servant's house for a great while to come." ii. Sam. vii. 18, 19. On the other hand, should his children not do as he would wish in their youth, he will be comforted that the covenant exhibited in their baptism, secures his own salvation and may yet effect their reformation even in old age. "Although my house be not so with God; yet he hath made with me an everlasting covenant, ordered in all things and sure, and this is all my salvation and all my desire, although he make it not to grow. ii. Sam. xxiii. 5. The parent's precepts and prayers may do good to the son, when the father has long been in the dust. Eccl. xi. 1. "Cast thy food upon

the waters ; for thou shalt find it after many
days." Prov. xxii. 6. " Train up a child in the
way he should go and when he is old he will not
depart from it?" What then? Shall the cavils of
controversy be allowed to cancel from the tabla-
tures of the Church, the bestowments of grace ?
Shall rude opposition without any reason, deprive
at once, the pious parent of his highest gratification, and rob God of his peculiar right? Shall
the sword of sophistry be drawn to sunder the
bonds of mutual duty, and divide the ligaments
of closest fellowship among the members of
Christ's body ? Shall any opponent of infants'
rights and covenant privileges dare sacrilegiously
to pillage from the Church, the pledges of her
permanency and future glory ? In vain. " The
mountains shall depart and the hills be removed,
but my kindness shall not depart from thee, neither shall the covenant of my peace be removed,
saith the Lord that hath mercy on thee.—All thy
children shall be taught of the Lord.—No weapon
that is formed against thee shall prosper, and every tongue that shall rise against thee in judgment thou shalt condemn. This is the heritage
of the servants of the Lord, and their righteousness is of me, saith the Lord." Shall the pillars
of hoary infirmity be broken down, and all the
balmy consolation of parental solicitude be torn
away from our New Testament sanctuary ? No ;
rather let the weakest stripling in the camp of
Israel, stand forth against the advocates of babes
than suffer venerable age to be thus insulted. If

from the dazzling glare of Jerusalem scenery you wish to recede ; if from the sublime heights of Zion and divine documents on her monuments inscribed, you wish to descend to the duskier vale of later story—Agreed. On that area, Providence concurring, we are prepared to shew that infants were baptized in the earliest ages of the Christian era, and that the right of the infants of regular church members to that ordinance, was not, till about the sixteenth century, by any religious body, or even respectable individual, disputed. In the mean time, we readily admit that, by adroit address, your system can be rendered plausible, and by unwearied and examplary assiduity it has been very successful. You are not, however, to suppose that certain victory awaits your cause by reason of the great accession of modern times. Number is tiny proof of any thing. In the present age and state of the Church, it is presumptive evidence of something else than truth or instituted piety. "The spirit speaketh expressly that in the latter times some should depart from the faith, giving heed to seducing spirits."—"This know also that in the last days perilous times shall come," &c.—"But there were false prophets also among the people, even as there shall be false teachers among you, who privily shall bring in damnable heresies, even denying the Lord that bought them, and bring upon themselves swift destruction, and *many* shall follow their pernicious ways, by reason of whom the way of truth shall be evil spoken of." 1 Tim. iv—ii. Tim. iii.

T 2

ii. Pet. ii. 1, 2. If you have the truth upon your side you need neither boast of numbers, nor fear the strongest armies which can be marshalled against your system. Truth will, in proper time, triumph. If you have not, you are not to suppose, that, by high pretensions, loud declamations, bold assertions, and fascinating hymns, you will prevail. With these remarks which, as they are candidly offered, I hope will be candidly received, I bid you, and all the truth you mantain, an affectionate—FAREWELL.

PART VI.

AN ADDRESS TO PEDOBAPTISTS.

————— ✳ —————

'AFTER a long excursion, I have, at last, arrived among you, whose practice I have been vindicating.

It is proper that you should not only know your authority for infant baptism and the legitimacy of its administration by affusion ; (both of which have been in modern times much controverted) but also, that you should know and seriously consider the duties belonging to, and the comforts accruing from, the right observation of this ordinance. A practical attention to the duties and privileges of this institution, we would earnestly urge upon you, both for the corroboration of the truth, and the experimental confirmation of the goodness of your cause, and the propriety of our plea.

To three classes we would direct this address.

1st. To parents, guardians or sponsors.

2dly. To children or youth.

3dly. To church officers.

So soon as infants are known to have life they become to the conscious parents characters in whose behalf, secret, frequent and fervent prayers should be offered. Every religious parent will be solicitous to have his child as soon and as visibly as possible under the guardianship of God and regimen of grace. Every mean is to be used. Neither adults when coming themselves nor infants brought by their parents have any merit to plead in their own behalf. But if they have God's promise of gracious acceptance that should encourage. "Whosoever cometh I will in no wise cast out." Fathers ought to shew a particular solicitude for the spiritual welfare of their baptized children. We may sin as much in respect of them as in respect of ourselves, in being more concerned about what they shall eat, and what they shall drink, than about their spiritual nourishment and growth in grace. What should we think of the man who would spend his son's estate on trinkets and gewgaws! What trinkets and trifling playthings are to an estate, that, and less, is an estate to a literary, scientific, and religious instruction. What an emphasis should be put upon that commandment, "Bring them up in the nurture and admonition of the Lord." The mother who fosters her infants should be particularly attentive to them. She should travail for them the second time, that they may be subjects of a second birth, and as soon as they are capable of knowing any thing, and that is sooner than many imagine, she ought frequently to press them to the breasts of christian and motherly affection, while she tells over and over to them, the all interesting tale of redeeming love.

' Let parents bewail, as they see it, that corrup-
tion which is entailed from father to son through
all the successive generations of man.   They will
have, by this means, an opportunity of seeing a
miniature representation of their own unchild-
like disposition and undutiful conduct.   By
teaching their children, parents and they become intellectually and morally knit together.
What a harmony and analogy may be traced between their natural and moral dependance ! By
this parents have a call to improve themselves in
christian knowledge.   They are called to mature,
and digest for communication, the rudiments of
piety and wisdom, which, in youth, they themselves studied.   By this they have a fine opportunity of doing good, and of enjoying delight.
What raptures of joy may not the parent allow
to swell his bosom, while, in obedience to the
divine and gracious arrangement, he brings up the
child for God, and so obtains a well grounded assurance that his offering has been accepted, and,
while he cherishes a joyous anticipation that after
a momentary separation, they shall see other
again where there shall be no more an infant of
days, decrepid age, or lugubrious mortality !
What overflowings of joy will be experienced in
that immortal state, when all the channels of good,
shall have converged, and become not distant,
but immediate pointers to the great and *present*
Source !   Then all terrestrial solicitude shall be
soothed into celestial serenity ;—all painful, parental cares shall be turned into confirmed joy ;

and children's waywardness into glorious adult liberty. It is a pretty sight, even here, to see the Father confidently laying aside the supercilious constriction of countenance, and caution of conduct, which must be, in some degree, maintained in the intercourse with his children, in juvenile life. The children, at the same time, without forgetting the reverence which they early learned to cherish toward their parents, yet venturing to assume, in conversation, a manly confidence. How exquisitely delightful to see them engage in counsels respecting the church; the son perhaps the better informed, yet willing to shew the greatest deference to his father's hoary hairs and sage experience !!! What heart can fail to feel pleasing emotions when such a scene presents itself? But O! how faint is the resemblance? Some may suppose that as there will be neither marrying nor giving in marriage in heaven, there will be there no relative affections.

To this I would say—1st. It is not an infirmity but a property of our social nature to love relatives, and I do not know that these properties of our social natures shall be effaced in our future and far more perfect state. 2dly. Grace does not weaken, but rather strengthens and improves our natural affections. What evidence is there, then, that grace consummated in glory will annihilate them? It is true, grace gives the love of God a supreme place, so that compared with this, a man must hate his child, his life; but this does not say that the love of children and life is less than before, but only that one is introduced which is greater. Charity is accumulative and perfecting of all benevolent affections, and while it teaches a lesson of active beneficence to all, especially to the household of faith, I know no precept, or principle of this permanent grace, that would forbid a peculiar complacency with our near relatives if they are with us heirs of the same covenant of promise and sharers of the same grace of eternal life. Genuine charity begins at home. "He that provideth not for his own, and especially for those of his own house, hath denied the faith and is worse than an infidel." This charity we have reason to believe "*never faileth.*" 3dly. Christ does not now lay aside his affection for his brethren; but says, " I will see you again, and your joy no man shall take away. All whom he draws he loves with an everlasting love; " whom he loves he loves to the end." He says —" Father, I will that they whom thou hast given me may be with me." Why may we not suppose that this same disposition has a place, to a certain degree, in the breasts of departed parents? Of course, when their children shall be brought home to the mansions of their forerunners, to the bosom of Abraham, to the social and celestial banquet of the holy patriarchs, will it not be a scene of delight? How differently will death be viewed by celestial and terrestrial parents! Are not these joys worth some pains? But should the picture be reversed, What sights, what sighs on

yonder side the gulph ? If reprobate rich glut-
tons cannot bear to see their profligate compan-
ions and brothers, how will faithless fathers bear
the sight of their ruined sons ? Harsher than the
infernal doors is the reverberating sound of their
mutual recriminations. " If God will pour out
his fury upon the heathen and upon the families,
generally, that call not upon his name"—" If all
the wicked and the nations that forget God shall
be turned into hell"—" if it shall be more tolerable for Sodom and Gomorrah, for Tyre and Sidon
than for Chorazin and Bethsaida, what must become of those families and cities that have been
taken visibly into covenant with God, and yet
have neglected their christian privileges and covenant duties ? We do not justify those who reject the counsel of God against themselves as
their offspring by refusing to submit to the baptismal rite and consequent ecclesiastical obligation ; nor do we pretend to say whether you that
are theoretically right and practically wrong, or
they who are wrong in both, will be most condemned before God ; but we are sure that a baptist is not so inconsistent, if he be careless of his
family, as you are. The scripture is itself explicit that he who knows the master's will and
does it not, shall be beaten with many stripes.
" Better not to vow, than to vow and not to pay."
To be sure, this latter will particularly apply to
things indifferent, among which the devotion of
our children to our God cannot be counted. If
there should be some among our Anabaptist op-

ponents, notwithstanding the paralysing system into which they have been seduced, who are con-scientious in educating their children, and some among you who are the contrary, the scripture has decided upon the case. The one says, " I will not, and yet goes ; the other—I' go, sir, and goes not." Were it not for instances of this kind the, right of infants to baptism would be easily main-tained. But alas! there are some who hold the truth in unrighteousness, and want nothing more for themselves or their offspring but the name of Christians, to take away their reproach, and in-stead of answering that end, it brings a reproach upon others and makes their own double. They are by this means not only breakers of the law of God, but of their own covenants and vows, also. To such we would say, Be consistent, deny religion altogether ; or strive, by the grace of God, to live according to its maxims, both in relation to yourselves, and your families. You will perhaps object—That you have not leisure to pay that attention to the religious education of your children, which according to christian rules and baptismal vows you ought. What is this? You have not leisure! That intimates that you have something of greater importance than your duty that engrosses your attention. You do not like that construction ; but of what other, turn it as you can, is it susceptible? And can you really, hope to succeed in worldly projects by breach of christian law, violation of covenant engagements, murder of your children's souls, and sacrilege

U

against God? Admit you can save half an hour
per day by neglecting the morning and evening
oblations, may you not soon loose more than that
in the dissipation of folly, debility of sickness, or
blasting of prospects by divine judgments, on account of this unbelieving and profane course? Religion is not an expenditure of time, nor calculated,
when rightly understood and practised, to injure
our worldly circumstances: Deut. 11. 6. "And
these words which I command thee this day shall
be in thine heart, and thou shalt teach them diligently unto thy children, and shalt talk of them
when thou sittest in thine house & when thou walk-
est by the way, & when thou liest down, and when
thou risest up." See the good effects, even in a
temporal view, which a compliance with this precept has, both in the connection of the passage
and in the history of that people to whom it was
first given. Either your plan upon which the objection is predicated, is wrong; or the scripture
is wrong, which represents "godliness as profitable in all things, having the promise of the life
that now is and of that which is to come."
i. Tim. iv. 8. "Godliness with contentment is
great gain." chap. vi. 6. But the negligent will
farther perhaps object—We have not ability to
teach our family to perform and observe the duties of religion as we ought. You are an humble
objector indeed; not able to teach your own children, ashamed to acknowledge the Saviour in acts
of religion before your own family!! But can
any man composedly and deliberately make this

objection and remember that he and his family
must die, and either be happy eternally in acts of
holiest worship in the presence of God ; or mis-
erable in eternal exclusion from God's presence,
with them that know not God and obey not the
gospel of Christ ?   Are you in jest, however, or
in earnest. : If the former, we would say to you.
Be not deceived ;. God is not mocked.   You
may. shield off the attacks of fellow mortals by
such pretexts and pretences, but how will you
answer God when he takes you to account ?   If
the latter, we would reply, In a certain sense, no
man is able for any thing, and in another sense,
every man is able for every thing.   Without
grace we can do nothing ; with it we can do all
things, "if ye believe all things are possible." -
If you feel incompetent to the task of religiously, educating your children, be diligent,
believing, and fervent. - Plead the promises . of
that very covenant which imposes upon you so
many necessary obligations.   Remember Truth
itself hath said, "If any of you lack wisdom, let
him ask of God, who giveth to all men liberally,
and upbraideth not ; *and it shall be given him.*"
James 1, 5.   "But he giveth more grace, wherefore he saith, God resisteth the proud and giveth
grace unto the humble. iv. 6, Humble yourselves
in the sight of the Lord and he shall lift you up."
ver. 10.   Do you yet object, that it will answer
no purpose without grace, as is evident from the
many instances of profligacy in religiously educated families? How evangelical you are !

We admit that Abraham's solicitude for Ishmael
did not hinder him to be a wild man ;—nor
Isaac's partiality for Esau reverse the counsel of
God to give the beloved Jacob the blessing and
ultimately the birthright ;—We admit that God's
sovereignty will be conspicuous, and the necessity of his gracious influence be manifested in all
things pertaining to salvation—" Paul may plant,
and Apollos water, it is God that must give the increase." What then ? Is Paul to cease sowing,
and Apollos to desist from watering ? Upon
your principle and mode of reasoning, that would
be the inference. It is evident you divide and
separate that which God hath joined, and you
virtually say, Unless you can effect something by
your own exertion without God's grace you will
do nothing. How pestilential and unholy your
principle; how unscriptural and unnatural your
maxim ? The scripture tells you, " Without me
ye can do nothing," and yet it inculcates duty.
You do not act upon your own maxim in natural
things. To set the folly and impiety of this objection in a clear light ; to illustrate and enforce
the duty of parents towards their children, I
avail myself of assistance from Wardlaw's Lec-
tures on Romans iv. 9—25. From this little, but
able piece, I might have extracted many pertinent
remarks on the grace of the Abrahamic covenant,
had I seen the book before that part was printed.
In his third lecture, after having shewn with
great perspicuity and force, 1. That there is no
absurdity in administering ordinances of spiritual

import to children. 2. That circumcision and
baptism signify the same thing, only the former
respected Messiah to come, the latter Christ
come. 3. That the Abrahamic covenant, which
was confirmed before of God in Christ, is the everlasting covenant under which we are, and, of
course, embraces infants. He then infers, p. 109
—" The charge entrusted to you, who bear the
character of parents, is the most solemnly important and tenderly interesting that can be imagin-
ed by the human mind. It is the charge of immortal souls. Every child that is born into the
world enters upon an existence that is never to
terminate ; upon a short life on the earth, which
must be succeeded by eternal blessedness or eternal woe. How affecting the consideration !
And with regard to your own children, to you is
committed the sacred trust of imparting to them
that knowledge which shall make them wise unto
salvation. These lights, lighted for eternity, it
is yours to feed with holy oil from the sanctuary
of God, that they may shine, forever in his presence, to his glory. The language of God to every Christian parent, is that of Pharoah's daughter
to the mother of Moses—" Take this child and
nurse it for me." Forget not, then, the sacred'
obligation. Let it be engraven on your hearts
as with a pen of iron, and the point of a diamond,
You love your children ; they are dear to you as
the apple of your eye—as your own souls—you
would part with any thing to secure their welfare.
And are not their eternal interests first in your

thoughts and first in your desires? If you feel
as Christians, they are, they must be. Let them
then, be first in your prayers, and first in your
exertions.—Seek to impress early on their hearts
a sense of the unspeakable importance of eternal
things. Teach them the knowledge of the Lord,
when you sit in the house, and when you walk
by the way; never with the repulsive authority
of a master, but with all the engaging tenderness
of parental love. Let no probability of temporal
advantage induce you to expose their souls to peculiar hazards from the temptations of this ensnaring world.—Let no accomplishments of body
or of mind, however gratifying and endearing
they may lawfully be, engross that particular joy,
which, in the hearts of Christian parents, will
ever be reserved for " seeing their children walking in the truth." Remembering that God alone
can give your desires their gratifications, and
your labours their increase, pray without ceasing,
that He may " pour out his Spirit upon your
seed and his blessing' upon your offspring; that
they may spring up as among the grass and as
willows by the water courses; and be a part of
the planting of the Lord, that he may be glorified." Present them, for a blessing, to that gracious Saviour, who said, in the days of his flesh,
" Suffer little children to come unto me and forbid them not, for of such is the kingdom of heav-
en." As Christians, it is a part of your experience that the promises of God do not operate as
encouragements to indolence, but as incentives to

activity.—You are stimulated to "work out your own salvation with fear and trembling," by considering that "it is God that worketh in you both to will and to do of his good pleasure." His declaration that "his people shall never perish," instead of lulling you in careless security, animates you, by banishing despair, "to gird up the loins of your minds," and to "run with patience the race that is set before you."—So, let the peculiar regard which God, in the promise of his covenant, has been shewn to have, to the offspring of his people, encourage you in discharging the duty of "bringing up your children in the nurture and admonition of the Lord." Let it inspire your prayers for them, with the animating confidence of expectation, and enliven your exertions with the hopes of success.

The connection is indissolubly established between the fulfilment of his promises on God's part, and attention to duty in the use of appointed means on the part of his people. To expect the one without the other, is not to trust in God, but unwarrantable presumption. Set your hearts with intense desire, on the salvation of your children;—Ask it of God, with the fervour and persevering importunity of faith. Shew the sincerity of your desires and prayers, by unwearied attention to the use of necessary means, and I doubt not, you will have the blessedness of seeing amongst your offspring a seed arise to serve the Lord.

Let the apparent failure of the blessing, in your

own families, or in those of other professing.
Christians, lead you rather to suspect yourselves
than to question the faithfulness of God. Such
cases, indeed, call to much searching of heart.—
Has the salvation of your children engaged your
desires with a fervour and constancy proportion-
ed to its infinite importance?—Have you pursued
this object with sufficient seriousness as the "one
thing needful" to your happiness as parents?
While you have been teaching the truths of God,
have you been careful to walk before your house
in a perfect way, exemplifing in your personal
behaviour, their holy, heavenly influence? Have
you, in no measure, been guilty of sacrificing the
souls of your children to temporal interest? Has
the object I speak of occupied that place in your
prayers and exertions to which its inconceivable
magnitude gives it so striking a claim?—Have
your prayers been the prayers of faith?—your
exertions believing exertions?—Or has there not
been, in both, a lamentable want of faith in God?
May the "God of all the families of Israel" lead
all believing parents to lay to heart, more deeply
than ever, the duty enjoined upon them! And
by bestowing an abundant blessing on parental
education, "instead of the fathers, take the children," that race unto race may praise him!"

Secondly. To children and youth who have
been baptized.

DEAR CHILDREN—In vindication of your
rights has this plea been exhibited. This book
has, therefore, upon your attention, a particular

claim, and that its publication may do you good, its author feels a peculiar solicitude, at the bar of a practical public. It may also be remarked, very much depends upon the conduct of the clients, and the apparent impression which the plea itself makes upon you whose cause it advocates. If you consider the matter at issue of small importance, who will be likely to take any great interest in the case. On the other hand, if it be found that you feel an early and a growing solicitude of living as free born citizens of Zion, and as early enfeoffed with great rights, high dignity, and an heavenly inheritance, few will then be so hardy as to oppose your covenant claims. It is true, He who has allowed you to be acknowledged heirs of such an inheritance, will not, on account of some childish foibles, have you disinherited. As appointed, however, a tutor of your minority, I would apprize you, that though you be children, you should reckon yourselves children of the light and of the day, who should not sleep as do others, but watch and be sober. So soon as you are mature in knowledge and piety, you will be cordially allowed to pass from the tutorage of a minor state—from the class of catechumens, to the class of adult members in the Church of God. In other things of infinitely less importance, you have an eager desire of progressing, and an ardent ambition to excel. You look before you, you long for every approaching epoch and climacteric of life; why are you not more anxious to grow in grace and in the knowledge of your Lord and Saviour Jesus Christ? Your age is peculiarly favorable for learning, and we take it for granted, that before you read this address, you have been initiated into the doctrines of salvation. Those catechetical compends by which you have been indoctrinated, may be to you of great and lasting advantages. That they may be so, however, you must be apprized that you have not done with your primers when you can recite them accurately by memory when asked, or even when you can ask and answer them in the solitude and solemnity of sable night. If you would derive from them real good, you must meditate much upon their import, refer them for proof to the unerring standard of God's holy word, and strive by grace to live according to their pious maxims. This will be a proper and profitable exercise in various ways and for several reasons. 1st. It will assist you in understanding both the scriptures and the catechisms. 2dly. It will teach you to look for precise and definite ideas and doctrines in the holy scriptures. The scriptures are read, and catechisms learned to very little purpose, when no attention is paid to signification. It is a killing thing to mind nothing but the letter. You must, therefore, observe the direction of the Saviour—" *Search* the scriptures, for in them ye think ye have eternal life, and they are they which testify of me." You must study to *know* wisdom and instruction, to *perceive* the words of understanding, to *receive* the instruction of wisdom. 3dly. By pursuing this course, you

will be referring to the proper source for religious knowledge, you will be appealing to the supreme standard of faith and ultimate tribunal of
doctrine. " To the law and to the testimony, if
they speak not according to this word, it is because there is no light in them." Some may
probably object, that, seeing the scriptures must
be the last umpire, why not study them first and
alone? This objection, however specious, is by
no means solid. It is contrary to the method
found expedient in the prosecution of all literary
and scientific attainments. Every person knows
the propriety of grammatical institutes and scientific syllabi, or outlines and brief compends of
the various branches of study. Would not the
man be thought either in jest or a fool who would
say all philosophy must be founded upon observation actually made upon nature, therefore all
books of philosophy are unnecessary and pernicious? The indolent slugglard and idle truant
might approve of the method, but we are sure
the true spirit of philosophy would testify against
it. The diligent student will avail himself of the
aid to be derived from the experience and observation of others, while he will also be forward and industrious to test other men's systems
by his own actual experiments, and thus, while the
idle saunterer, following the path of the savage,
will make no improvement, the industrious student will obtain a rich feast from every scene of
nature, which passes under his intelligent review,
and, while he compares the natural original with

the artificial portrait of scientific system, will, doubtless, acknowledge the superlative grandeur and inimitable excellency of the former, will, at the same time, with modesty, and perfect consistency, admit the utility of the latter. The application of all this to the case in hand is easy. The Jewish scripturian—the Papist traditionist —the skeptical infidel—the wrangling bigot—the superstitous formalist—the enthusiastic fanatic, all steer courses, not *more* different from one another, than the true Christian. He will not be so silly as to suppose that much advantage is to be obtained by counting the words and letter of the inspired books, nor will he calculate much upon the phylacteries, talismans and amulets of scripture, thus profaned by the veiled Hebrew. Neither will he spend time in counting the feuds which recal to the mind of the catholic the name and fantastic deeds of canonized heroes, and tutelary saints, and imaginary mediators. He will not implicitly believe the *ipse dixits* of Popes, cardinals, and doctors ; neither will he for pride or interest, subscribe and maintain the creeds of councils, nor will he think himself certainly correct, when regulated in his conduct by the canons of hierarchial clergy. No ; while he may transiently glance at all this gilded trumpery, he will, with peculiar pleasure, and profit too, meditate upon God's law, and study the deep thoughts of the Spirit of Truth. He will, at the same time, avail himself of all the helps which the pious study and faithful testimony of ancient witnesses

afford. He will distinguish between the scriptures, which are God's testimony to men, and
the confessions of the faithful, which are the testimony of the Church for the cause of a redeeming God, exhibited before the eyes of a blind and
rebellious world. But I must hasten to a fourth
reason for, and use of, proving your rudiments of
early instruction by the word of God. It is evident if your word be correct it will have many
opponents. If it has not, it cannot be either
scriptural or true. This is the time, in which
men heap to themselves teachers having itching
ears. Many shall follow their pernicious ways,
by reason of which the way of truth shall be evil
spoken of. It is quite natural to suppose that
those teachers, who know not what themselves
say, nor whereof they affirm, who have no system, teach no doctrine, should wish to have auditors of a corresponding character. Such teachers as make once or twice crying to be conver-
sion, and going under the water to be obedience
to the gospel, certainly act consistently and pru-
dently, when they use all their influence to expel
from the christian world those forms of sound
words, which are calculated to assist the young
members of the church to understand the ora-
cles of God. Adults in years and infants in
knowledge are their best game, because they are
most easily affected and most readily persuaded
of a system which appears best with candle light.
If then, against the assaults of such cavillers as
want no other reason to oppose a doctrine, than

W

that it is contained in a catechism or confession of faith, you would be successful, you must connect two precepts of Paul to his son Timothy. In the first chapter, 13th verse, he exhorts him—— " Hold fast the form of sound words which thou hast heard of me, in faith and love which is in Christ Jesus," and in the third chapter of the same second epistle, 14th and 15th verses, he shews how this against seducers may be done—— "But continue thou in the things which thou hast learned and hast been assurred of, knowing of whom thou hast learned them : and, that from a child thou hast known the holy scriptures, which are able to make thee wise unto salvation through faith which is in Christ Jesus. Nearly related to this duty of intelligent and constant maintenance of the principles of truth, in which you have been taught, and intimately connected with its success will be a practical regard to the duties, which their doctrines and the precepts of your parents inculcate. Religion is not a mere theory ; the gospel of Christ must be *obeyed* If this fact and principle be not observed, the consequences will be doleful as the neglect is baneful. We are very apt to reckon our conduct reasonable, and always disposed to stand up in its defence. If, therefore, it should unfortunotely happen, my dear young friends, that your conduct and your creed should be found at variance, it will be at least matter of fear and doubt with those who wish your everlasting welfare, that you will renounce your orthodox faith rather than reform your heretical practice. Indeed, if sovereign grace prevent not, it will require no extraordinary sagacity to divine in such a case what will be the result. On the other hand, if you make conscience of conformity to the holy precepts of religion your faith will be strengthened, and your knowledge greatly increased. *"If you do the will of God, ye shall know of the doctrine whether it be of God."* What matter of rejoicing will it be to all your instructors if it be found that from the heart you obey that form of doctrine which has been delivered to you." Rom. vi. 17. Your pious parents will affectionately adopt the language of David. "And thou, Solomon my son, know thou the God of thy fathers. Thou shalt avouch the Lord to be thy God and thou shalt walk in his statutes and keep his commandments and do them." If God so peremptorily command you to obey your parents in all things, is it possible that you can with impunity be disobedient to these commandments which are in their nature so solemn and important? Your circumcision will be greatly profitable if you *keep* the law, but it had been better for you that you had been born Hottentots, Turks or Indians than that after having known the will of God, you be found to *turn away from the holy commandments.* Would you be successful in worldly things, this is your most political course, and we fear not the charge of legality in urging this as a motion, because we have abundance of scriptural precedent. "Seek ye first the kingdom of God and his righteousness and all these things shall be added unto you." Matt. vi. 33.' "Children obey your parents in the Lord for this is right. Honour thy father and thy mother, which is the first commandment with promise, that it may be well with thee, and that thou mayest live long on the earth." Eph. vi. 1, 2, 3. Surely if parents generally are to be honoured and obeyed in all common things, much more should *religious* parents be honoured and obeyed in *religious* things. "The eye that mocketh at his father and despiseth to observe the law of his mother the ravens of the valley shall pluck it out and the young eagle shall eat it." It must be admitted that you can, if you will, prevail in backsliding and apostacy against all the prayers and pains of parents and pastors ; but is it not possible that you may, in the end, be filled with your own ways ? Rather is it possible that you can wound the breasts, and wring the hearts of your religious friends with impunity ? Even could you, would you, thus requite the Lord of hosts ? 'Ah, foolish children, think not to strive with the Almighty. He will have a seed to do him service if some, even of the children of the kingdom, should be cast out. He will bring them from the north and the south, from the east and the west to sit down with Abraham : what will you then think ? Do you not now devoutly pray that you may be of the number of those sons whom he shall bring from afar, and of those daughters whom he shall bring from the ends of the earth ? Cease not, dear youth, thus to pray,

say—Art thou not our father? Having been
early enrolled among the disciples of Jesus Christ
see that you make early preparation to remember
that wonderful price which he paid as the ransom
of his children.   You will surely not consider the
dying command of the great Redeemer a *little*
one "Do this in remembrance of me." Is it
then a fact that whosoever breaketh the least of
his commandments, and teacheth men so shall be
called the least in the kingdom of heaven, what
then shall he be called that breaketh the greatest? Was it death under the Jewish economy
to omit the celebration of the paschal feast, can it
be a matter of little moment, whether or not we
keep that feast which is come in its room? You
fear unworthy communion; is there no danger of
obstinate neglect? You say, being unregenerated
you will eat and drink judgment to yourselves,
so you might if regenerate, as is clear from the
passage alluded to: But have you no fear to eat
a common meal? is there no danger that your
common table may be made a snare and a trap?
May not God, while you continue to slight his
invitations, and cast his commandments behind
your back, curse all your blessing? You are in
a predicament, from which nothing but divine
grace can extricate you. Why will you not then
yield to gracious offers, and cry for gracious and
divine influence? When in his word he says,
seek my face, say ye, Thy face Lord will we
seek; I will take of the cup of salvation and call
upon the name, yes, the saving name of the Lord.

You must remember too that every one that nam--
eth the name of Jesus must depart from iniquity.
Would it not be a horrid thing to turn the grace
of God into lasciviousness, and to trample under
foot the blood of the covenant. See then, that
you flee youthful lusts that war against the soul.
Be assured that if ye live after the flesh ye shall
die, but if ye through the Spirit do mortify the
deeds of the body ye shall live. You must consider yourselves as the property of Christ, as redeemed not with corruptible things as of silver
and gold from your vain conversation, and you
must then live to him and offer your souls and
your bodies living sacrifices, holy and acceptable,
which, as it is a reasonable service, so we can assure you it will be found, by all who seriously engage in it, a pleasant service. "Wherefore gird up
the loins of your mind, be sober and hope to the
end, for the grace that is to be brought unto you
at the revelation of Jesus Christ : as *obedient
children*, not fashioning yourselves according to
the former lusts, in your ignorance ; but as he
who hath called you is holy, so be ye holy in all
manner of conversation." "Little children keep
yourselves from idols."—As new born babes desire the sincere milk of the word that ye may
grow thereby. "Ye therefore, beloved, seeing
ye know these things before, beware lest ye also,
being led away with the error of the wicked, fall
from your own steadfastness. But grow in grace
and in the knowledge of our Lord and Saviour
Jesus Christ. To him be glory both now and
 ever.—Amen."

Thirdly, and finally—"The elders which are among you I exhort who am also an elder."

It must appear, even from the imperfect exhibition given in the foregoing parts of this plea, that the controversy between us and our Anabaptist professors is one of great and practical importance. Let us then be intelligently, practically, and unitedly decisive in its maintenance. If He, upon whose shoulders hang the keys of sole supremacy, allow children to be members of his church and kingdom, it cannot, for a moment, be questioned that we should catch the spirit of this wise, gracious and condescending arrangement, and should, of course, treat them as such. It must be pleasing to all the lovers of order and consistency in the Church, that the controversy about the half way covenant is now pretty much settled. I believe there are now but few in this country who would risque so far their reputation as to say, that openly wicked and irreligious men, who have evidently themselves no part in the matter, who have evidently rejected the counsel of God against themselves, should have baptism for their offspring. It is certainly, notwithstanding this, much to be regretted that sufficient care is not taken yet to seperate between the precious and the vile. We should remember that we are not the servants of men in the administration of doctrine, discipline and sacraments in the house of God, (however gratifying it may be to some to have a name for themselves and their's) if they want nothing more, it cannot be profitable to them,

but the contrary. What? shall we indulge them
in the dangerous gratification of profaning the
holy things of God's sanctuary! It may, I admit, conduce to our popularity, ease and affluence
thus to trifle and please men, saying, Peace, peace,
when there is no peace ; but shall we not be called to account for our stewardship? What shall
we servants answer the Lord of the house if we
are not faithful? I humbly submit another thing
to your consideration, *viz.* Whether our language
and conduct be correct concerning the children of
those parents, of whom we have good reason to
believe that they hold the promise precious,
which is to them and to their children. We profess an abhorrence of the system, which throws
the children of God's covenant people among the
dogs and sorcerers, and whoremongers, and murderers and idolators, and whosoever loveth and
maketh a lie, who are without.—We profess, to
oppose the system which hangs the children of
God's people upon the threshold of the church as
neither in the house nor out of the house. How
is it then that we talk about such when they are
grown up as if they were not members of the
Church, even before there has been any discipline
exercised upon them to cast them out? Why do
we talk of taking them into the Church, if they
were in it already? We say in our arguments
with those who oppose the membership of infants,
that they are members though yet but babes, and
of course, are only fed with the milk of plain doctrine and catechetical instruction in their junior

ity, Why then do we even seem to contradict this in our mode of speaking about them when they become strong, as we hope, for the stronger viands of sacramental food? If they are visibly engrafted into Christ by baptism, we should not afterwards speak of their joining the Church. If they are not, what is their baptism? It really does seem to me that either our language, or our conduct is incorrect. Do we not give too much ground for the enemies of infant membership to blaspheme the solemn rite of their presentation before the Lord and recognition as members of the Church? Might I submit another thing, dear brethren, to your consideration. I would ask, What should we do when a person who has never been baptized makes application for admission and shews a predeliction for immersion? Should we not tell such a person that although Pedobaptist Churches do not hold the mode to be very essential, that yet sprinkling is the common custom, and that of course if he thinks so too, it will not be his duty by schismatical obstinacy to destroy the uniformity of ecclesiastical ritual, especially in a day of so much dissension? If he says that he considers this the only scriptural mode then we certainly give neither him, nor the society of dippers, any justice if we take the job out of their hands. They are more expert in imposing this yoke upon Christ's disciples than we are, and should, of course, do it. I admit, there may be instances, in which we should have the list of our accessions, by this decisive practice

diminished; but this is no proof that the cause
of Pedobaptism would be thereby weakened.
To act otherwise would be horridly cruel to the
applicant himself. The man might then, it is true,
be satisfied that he had the ordinance purely and
properly administered to himself; but what
must he think of his father and his brethren?
The former he must consider ignorant or wicked
in the ordinary way of his administration of this
ordinance, and the latter as well as the former
unbaptized. Of course when he begins to reflect
upon these things he will, if he has any conscience,
or any consistence, join those who are properly
his brethren: I need hardly now ask, what should
we do if any should shew a desire, after having
been sprinkled, of being re-baptized by immersion, certainly no man will think himself justified
in profaning the name and ordinance of God by
unnecessary repetition, because of ignorant scruples. If these can, by scriptural argument and
christian remonstrance, be removed, well; if not
we must say as the Apostle about the distinguishing garb of males and females. 1 Cor. xi. 16.
" But, if any man seem to be contentious, we
have no such custom, neither the churches of
God." From these remarks a question may naturally arise, How is the membership of baptized
youth to influence our practice towards them?
The answer is ready, and we think obvious, viz.
We should consider them peculiarly under our
tuition and inspection. We should strive, by instruction and admonition to do good to all, but

·there should be an "especially" prefixed to the
" household of faith." We who are teaching elders should as bishops be apt to teach, we should
be ready in season and out of season to reprove,
rebuke and exhort, with all meekness, long suffering and doctrine—we should preach the gospel,
in short, to every creature, but we have a particular charge from the great Shepherd and Bishop
of our souls to " *Feed his lambs.*" When he ascended up on high he received gifts for men, and
gave some apostles, some prophets, (which were
extraordinary offices) and some pastors and
teachers for the edification of his Church. It is
evident that during their early infancy and youth
we must exercise our official trust upon them
chiefly through the medium of their parents.
But I know no reason why they, when grown up,
should be considered exempt from the immediate
exercise of that authority which we have received not for destruction, but for edification. It is
pleasing to know that several of the most conscientious clergy in the Reformed Dutch Church,
and in the General Assembly of the Presbyterian
Church have recently expressed their decided
approbation of this course of consistent and faithful discipline towards the young and interesting
members, and hope of the Redeemer's Church.
It would seem strange indeed that discipline
should be altogether omitted, in that very period
of life, when it is most likely to have a good effect: and equally strange, that they might indulge
in any excess of youthful folly with impunity, if

they have only the discretion to neglect the solemn duty of communion in the Lord's supper ! ! This must certainly be considered the very climax of practical absurdity, and yet, which of us can plead, in regard to it, innocence. Dear brethren, let us pray for one another that we may all become more conscientious and consistent; and let us co-oporate with one another, and strive together, that we may be more successful in producing practical reformation in the congregation of our charge. There is another thing. I wish the officers in Pedobaptist churches to study, *viz.* Is it proper that we should solicit Anabaptists to hold with us promiscuous fellowship in the Lord's supper? In relation to this question, it is much to be regretted, that we cannot be unanimous in opinion, and uniform in practice. There are two classes of characters who will be at no loss to decide all controversies of this kind. The bigotted partizan, on all such questions, decides at once. " They differ from us, we shall have nothing to do with them." The effeminate latitudinarian, who regulates all affairs of this kind by blind feeling, will answer such questions with equal promptness—" To refuse them fellowship, or to omit inviting them would be uncharitable." The intelligent Christian will be satisfied with neither of these modes of disposing of this question, he will say, in regard of the first, What? have nothing to do with a fellow-creature, and perhaps as well as myself, a christian ! With respect to the latter he would be at no loss to coincide, provided he were sure that charity requires us to hold communion with Anabaptists. All things should be done in charity. We should have charity not only towards all professors, but towards all men. But this does not say that we should blindly suppose that all men, unbelievers and wicked as well as others, will be saved; or that in our profession we should have no regard to orthodoxy any more than to heresy; or that we should make no distinction between orderly and disorderly brethren. The man who wishes to be a consistent christian, will view this subject in relation to the Anabaptists themselves. He will at once see that the most orthodox and orderly of that people, are opposed to catholic and unprincipled communion. With the Calvinistic and regular Baptists, then, the matter is generally known to be settled by themselves. Is it a matter, then, that merits much discussion, whether or not, we should amalgamate in profession with with those who, laying the controversy of baptism aside, deny the divinity of Christ, and set up the idol of the human will against the throne of divine grace? He must be libertine in principle, who with such would court communion. The true christian, who has had a humbling sense of his great depravity and sin, knows that none can be his saviour but God; of course, with those who have a Saviour less, or other than God, he cannot have communion. It would be cruel to ask those who are, in other things, pretty sound and order-

X

ly, Would we ourselves admit the unbaptized?
or those whom we deemed unbaptized ? If not,
then do we not act cruelly and contrary to our
Saviour's rule, if we ask them to do what we
could not, in like case, do ourselves? Suppose
the Quaker only to reject the one of the seals,
viz. baptism; would we in that case, while he
continued to reject the counsel of God requiring
him to be baptized; would we, I say, bolster up
his presumption, and encourage him in his rebellion, by sealing to him in the supper, as far as we
could, his right to everlasting peace and blessedness? Surely no, we could not be so cruel.   The
Baptists look on us, however, in the same light
as we would these supposed Quakers. Is it not
then cruel in us to ask them for communion, until
we persuade them that we are baptized? But,
again—Should we with candour contemplate the
matter as respects ourselves, we ought not to be
proud, neither should we allow any to despise either ourselves or our system.   What then is likely to be the conclusion that the considerate will
draw, when all the objection which is heard against
Anabaptists is, that they will not fellowship us?
Will it not be that they are conscious of being
right, and are consistent, while we have no conscience about the matter, only to court popularity
and make members to our own society? Whatever temporary and local effect the loose method
may produce in favour of a political man who
dexterously manages momentary circumstances,
it will be seen that this loose method will, in the

end, weaken the cause of its advocates. It is, therefore, upon a large scale 'impolitic as well as we have before shewn it to be' cruel.' It is also mean. The Anabaptists call us unbaptized and yet we will ask of them sealing privileges ; as if either our edification or comfort were 'dependant upon their favour. We should, I know, study meekness, but 'I do not know that we should cultivate meanness. Finally, it is unfaithful. Are we stewards and bound to separate between the precious and vile ? Is the chaff; then, of their dreams and notions to be mixed with the truth of a pure profession ? Are we watchmen ? and ought we not to give an alarm, when any dangerous hostile error approaches the walls of our Jerusalem ? Can we do this, and at the same time, admit them to all the solemnities of our holy communion, and inmost sanctuary? Have we no altar, to which they have no right who serve the tabernacle ? Are we soldiers, yea ensigns under Jesus, our great Captain? Are we not therefore bound, when errors break in as a flood to lift up a banner against them. It is true, if our personal enemy hungers, we should feed him with the bread of hospitality at our own tables, but I know no authority we have to feed the enemies of truth and christian peace at the table of the Lord. On the contrary, if we would be faithful we must "mark them who cause divisions contrary to the doctrines which we have received, and avoid them.* The truth is, none on either

* Rom. xvi. 17.

side that are fully persuaded and conscientious, will be fond of this promiscuous and unprincipled fellowship. They knew that, in existing circumstances, they must count each other disorderly and so, even if they do reckon each other brothers, they must withdraw because of supposed disorderly walking, " Can two walk together except they be agreed."† If we would have communion together which will be edifying and permanently comfortable, it must be on the consistent basis of union, and that union must be predicated upon the permanent basis of truth. * ' Love the truth and the peace." †" What fellowship hath light with darkness?" Certainly, if the one of the systems be righteousness, the other in its opposition must be unrighteousness; and then there cannot be fellowship. If the one be light the other must be darkness, and so there cannot be communion. Do then, let us be faithful and consistent, and not put the invention of our opponents so far to the rack as to oblige them to assert, that the Apostles had not Christian baptism, in order to justify themselves in inviting or in admitting us. If we have the truth, we need not have recourse to any indirect and unfaithful means to obtain professors of it. The God of truth will influence, by his Spirit, to this whom he pleases. Let us, under the influence of that assurance, use with diligence all the means which he puts in our power, and which the genius of his kingdom admits. Let us strive to have

† Amos iii. 3. * Zech. viii. 19. ‡ 2 Cor. vi. 14.

our people well instructed, especially in all present truth. Let us concur with each other, as far as we are agreed, in giving to truth its proper effect upon the conscience and conduct of men: Let us be particularly diligent in feeding the lambs of the Redeemer's flock. I am persuaded that an intelligent pastor will have no greater joy in any part of his charge, than in concurring with his clement Master in the gracious work of gathering them in his arms and carrying them in his bosom. I think I may safely say for all my Pædobaptist brethren in the ministry, that, when they drink largely of their Master's spirit, there is no part of their labour, in which they have more countenance and more comfort, than in witnessing and ministering in the dedication of babes to Jesus, whom they still hear from above the mercy seat, saying, "Suffer little children, and forbid them not, to come unto me, for of such is the kingdom of heaven." May I not also appeal to you, if towards these dear children of the kingdom it be not most congenial to a pastor's heart, to cherish, under the influence of grace, the strongest affection and tenderest solicitude? Let us concur with their parents in presenting them with faith and fervent love to the Saviour of his children, and although we may be sometimes called in this work to sow in tears of solicitude we shall have a reaping time of joy. Although in the dispensation of the concerns of the world and the Church, there may be, in the present state of things, much suffering connected with the relations which cause most exquisite joy, yet in the end, if we are faithful, we shall have happiness without mixture, measure or end. What must be the emotions, the extacy, the beatitude of faithful pastors, when called to shew with the chief Shepherd in that moment of Mediatorial exultation, when he will say, " Here am I, and the children whom thou hast given me?" Compared with the felicity of that hour, what are the joys of momentary marriage? what the triumphs of temporary victory? what the splendours of fading crowns? what the glory of a dissolving world?!!

PART IV.

AN ADDRESS TO THE UNDETERMINED.

———— ✳ ————

THESE may be arranged into three classes.

1st. Such as have descended from Anabaptist parents, and of course, as far as education extends its influence, are prepossessed in favour of that system, though yet undetermined.

2d. Such as have been brought up to no religion at all, and perhaps are skeptical about all.

3d. Such as have been baptized in infancy, and yet are, by Anabaptist arguments, induced to waver.

With you of the first class, I feel myself bound to treat upon the subject with the greatest sympathy and tenderness, because, however incorrect the system of our fathers may be, it deserves, on their account, some considerable support. Children are naturally disposed to credit what their parents say and believe. All their early views of religious things are derived through the channel of their instructions, and it really seems to me that in the precept, "Children obey your parents" is implied, that we should be of their religion unless upon very mature reflection and conscientious

investigation of the scriptures, we discover a better. To an age of so much revolutionary enter-
prize as the present, and to the descendants of a
people of so much missionary exertion and proselyting zeal as your ancestors have always cher-
ished- we need hardly state that the religion
even of our fathers should be examined by the
supreme standard; and if in this balance it be
found wanting, should be abandoned. If this
principle be denied, how are we to justify the
spirit and practice of the Reformers of the ever
memorable 16th century, who shook, in the continent of Europe, the old establishments of papal
domination, superstition and idolatry ? In what
darkness had we been groping, in what distress
involved, had they revered the religion of their
fathers above the religion of God's word ? Nay,
how could we justify the practice of Christ's own
Apostles, who reasoned and testified against the
sayings and traditions of old times, who displayed the banner of truth and sounded loud and
long the trump of war against all the systems of
religion which were then formidable by the multitude of their advocates, and venerable by the
sages of antiquity who had been active in their
establishment. Of all youth, it may also be remarked, you have the strongest inducements to be
candid and disinterested in your investigations of
this description. The system of your fathers
has taught them to cast you, in religious matters,
at the door of public pity. Though the children
of those whom they consider almost exclusively

christian, they have excluded you from the church
and pronounced you no more worthy of a place
in the house of God, than the cattle of the hovel
or the hogs of the sty. Still we would not have
you forgetful of the kindness of your parents in
the exercise of care over, and kindness to, your
bodies. Give the system they defend a candid
and careful examination, and if you find that
they were authorized by the head of the Church
to exclude you from his kingdom, let them have
credit and do likewise. But if, on the contrary,
you find that Christ allows parents to bring their
children to him for a blessing and a public recognition as members of the kingdom of heaven, we
would, for the sake of your offspring and for the
honour of the Redeemer's clemency and condescension and mercy, entreat you to lay aside the
ignorant zeal which has deprived you of the honour and advantage of early adoption into the number and privileges of the family of God. Preserve the same course in this case as you would,
without any advice, in a political concern of a
similar kind. Suppose your parents had been in
the lot of the patriotic heroes who, under the protection and auspices of the Almighty, achieved
the liberty of this much favoured land, and by
their gallant exploits with their compatriots in
arms, obtained the franchise of citizens in this
commonwealth; yet not understanding the generous principles of the constitution in this respect,
through mistake, had excluded you from the inheritance of soldier's lands and freemen's rights,

saying you had no more right to these, possessions and this freedom than the children of red
Indians or sable Hottentots, What in this case
would you do? Would you not say, certainly
our parents designed us no harm, but they reasoned incorrectly. The question relative to us
was not, whether we had any personal merit, or
desert of gallant deed, according to their own
tenure of these privileges, but whether the consti-
tutional charter allows us, as their children, calculating charitably that we would be worthy of such
ancestors, to inherit their possessions and liber-
ties, until we forfeit them by actual misdemeanor.
Having discovered this mistake, would you not
give in the names of your children, have them
enrolled as citizens, and so endowed with all the
privileges competent to their age? Would you
not teach them to say to those who would question their rights, as Paul said, " Yes, but I was
free-born"? Should you act otherwise, you
would not only injure your children, but also
prolong the evil accruing, from the ignorance of
your parents. By their mistake their children
were denied of a privilege, but by your continuance in their system you would make them to
blame for the disfranchisement of their grand-
children. Should you say the cases are not similar; Christ's kingdom is not of this world, we
would so far admit that its genius is, in many respects different : It is not established by intrigue
nor perpetuated by force and cruelty ; but are you
really prepared to say that the covenant of grace,

the charter of the commonwealth of Israel, is inferior to the constitution of the nations and kingdoms of this world in clemency and mercy?
No; you shudder at the thought. You would
not even admit that the dispensation of this covenant in the New Testament is behind, in clemency, the same dispensation as it respected the
church in the wilderness, or as it was displayed
in the ecclesiastical establishment of God's ancient Israel. Admitting this then, can you doubt
that the blessing of Abraham should visibly descend upon the seed of the Gentile Church?
This way of arguing will, I know, have no influence upon your conduct, if you believe the cavils
of half bred deists, who deny and ridicule the
first and largest part of the Bible; if there was
no covenant of grace nor Church of the redeemed till the commencement of the present era, then
we must admit that from the scriptures of ancient
times and the dispensation of God toward the
fathers, nothing can be learned. If Christ came
to destroy the law and the prophets, to abrogate,
while sojourning in the flesh, and suffering on
the cross, the promises which were before confirmed of God in Christ to the fathers, then indeed we shall despair of influencing you any
thing by our plea in behalf of your own rights
and the rights of your descendants. If you can
believe that the promise " He will be your God
and the God of your seed" meant nothing more
than that "if they behave well according to the
political statutes of this time, they and their's

should possess the land of Palestine, I shall, indeed despair of effecting any thing by my arguments. If, on the contrary, you should take a view of the God of Israel as the same merciful God, with whom the members of the Church have yet to do, of Jesus Christ as the same yesterday, to day and forever, of the covenant of grace as the covenant which was established upon a basis, more permanent than the mountains which may be removed, then we shall hope, that you will believe that the promise is to you and *to your children*, and that you will be baptized with all *yours* straightway, resolving that whatever others do, as for you and your houses you will serve the Lord. You need not be afraid of calculating too largely upon God's constant and consistent clemency. He proposes to you now the same covenant that he proposed by Isaiah lv. chap. " I will make with you an everlasting covenant, ordered in all things and sure, for it was even the sure mercies of David." As the heavens are higher than the earth, so are his ways and thoughts higher than ours. You may see what these sure mercies of David are by turning your attention to the lxxi and lxxix Psalm—" O God, thou hast taught me from my youth ; and hitherto have I declared thy wondrous works. Now also, when I am old and grayheaded, O God, forsake me not, until I have shewed thy strength unto this generation, and thy power to every one that is to come." " But my faithfulness and my mercy shall be with him, and in my name shall his

horn be exalted. I will set his hand in the sea,
and his right hand in the rivers. He shall cry
unto me, Thou art my father, my son, and the
rock of my salvation. Also I will make him my
first born, higher than the kings of the earth. My
mercy will I keep for him forevermore, and my
covenant shall stand fast with him. *His seed* also will I make to endure forever, and his throne
as the days of heaven—Once have I swore by my
holiness that I will not lie unto David. His *seed*
shall endure forever, and his throne as the sun
before me." If this gracious and everlasting
covenant be all your salvation and desire, you will
no doubt desire to have it sealed in the most decent, expressive, and scriptural manner. You will
remember that it was really sealed by the effusion
of the blood of Christ. Although the system of
your parents has hindered the early application of
the symbol, the promise yet continues to address
you: I will sprinkle clean water upon you, from
all your filthiness and from all your idols will I
cleanse you. I will pour water upon him that is
thirsty, and floods upon the dry ground. I will
pour my spirit upon thy seed, and my blessing
upon thy offspring * However men and systems
may do for a while, God will accomplish his
word, and will proselyte the nations in that way
which shall commemorate best the great deed of
the Redeemer's death, when his face was sprinkled with blood running from his temples, pierced

* Isa. xliv 3.

Y

with the thorny crown : " As many were astonished at thee ; his visage was so marred more
than any man, and his form more than the sons
of men : *so shall he sprinkle many nations ;* the
kings shall shut their mouths at him ; for that
which had not been told them shall they see, and
that which they had not heard shall they consider.* In these happy times there shall be one
great ecclesiastical establishment, which will embrace the world, young and old, the kingdoms of
this world shall become the kingdoms of Christ.
He will then reign over his saints in Jerusalem and
to the ends of the earth.   It is true children shall
then have an admirable maturity of understanding and perhaps none of them will be called hence
in infancy.   Then " they shall not labour in
vain, nor bring forth for trouble ; for they are the
seed of the blessed of the Lord, AND THEIR OFF-
SPRING WITH THEM."†   In that happy state of
society the Church shall have no more trouble
with the Canaanite in the house of the Lord of
hosts, they shall then be rid of *strange* children ;
yet for the building and ornament of that spacious
and glorious temple of the Millenial Church, sons
shall be plants, and daughters fair carved stones.
" Rid me and deliver me from the hand of strange
children whose mouth speaketh vanity, and whose
right hand is a right hand of falsehood, that *our
sons* may be as plants grown up in their *youth ;*
that our daughters may be as corner stones pol-
ished after the similitude of a palace ; that our

* Isa liv 14, 15.   † Isa. lxv. 23.

garners may be full, affording all manner of store : that our sheep may bring forth thousands and ten thousands in our streets : that our oxen may be strong to labor, that there be no breaking in, nor going out ; that there be no complaining in our streets. *Happy is that people that is in such a case : yea, happy is that people whose God is Jehovah.*"*

To the second class, who have been brought up to no religion at all.

There is one thing of which all of this general class should take diligent heed, viz. That they do not consider points which are made matters of controversy, to be therefore indifferent. Upon this principle, what could be considered essential ? Not only the truth of the scriptures, but also the being of a God has been questioned. Whether they are practically and pretendedly Atheists, or also speculatively and in their deliberate opinions, may itself be matter of controversy, and upon this men high in the estimation of the Church have already decided differently : but, that they are Atheists their words and their works conspire to prove. Men too have had different views—hot and bloody controversies about the best mode of civil polity. Does this prove that there is no difference what kind of government men adopt, or that they may do as well without any, and live in a state of confusion and anarchy ? Such differences may render delay necessary ; because the discussion may require time ; but no

* Psalm cxiv. 11, 12, 13, 14, 15.

prudent man will think that general skepticism
is thereby justified ; or that permanent discon-
nection with every society is therefore proper or
safe. Although the diversity of opinion may occasion some disagreeable feeling both to parties
regularly organized and to enquirers ; yet the
man who has a real desire to know the truth, will
thankfully improve the opportunity which collis-
ion affords to examine opinions and elicit truth.
This is, doubtless, the improvement we should
make of the present divisions among professors.
" Many shall run to and fro and knowledge shall
be increased." In your deliberations and investigations it will be necessary for you to distinguish
between facts and inferences, first principles and
conclusions. Upon the former you will find as
much argument in the evidence as is necessary in
order to form a fair verdict. The chicanery of
advocates will in all trials clash ; if you can bring
principles of law to bear upon authentic facts of
evidence, you will then be prepared to decide.
The bible is before you containing the solemn
depositions of competent, disinterested, yea self
denied and devoted evidences. There is certainly something very peculiar in the character of
these witnesses and of their testimony. There is
an inimitable majesty and fidelity in the former
and consistency in the latter which can be accounted for on no other principle, but upon the majesty and force of truth. And then you are to remember that they relate miracles, which had they
not happened, could be easily confuted.. They

court no men's favour or concurrence. Moses
relates the miracles of God and the obduracy of
the people, his own rashness and dies. The
prophets reprove and are hated, rejected and slain;
and yet the murderers of these prophets declare
the truth of their prophecy and garnish their
tombs. In their narratives there is evidently no
collusion in order to be consistent with each other, and yet when carefully examined they all agree.
As there is no way to account for the existence of
the scriptures but that they are divine revelation;
so, there is no way to account for the existence of
a true Church but that its members are influenced to join it by the Divine Spirit. The scriptures and the Church unite in testifying of Jesus
as the seed of the woman, who was to appear in
our nation. In the beginning of this era the scep-
tre having departed from Judah, and that land
having become a Roman province, Jesus was
born at Bethlehem. That primary fact then is
admitted by both. The Jew says, however, that
he was an illegitimate child, for both Jews and
Christians agree that he was not the son of Joseph. For Mary conceived before they came together. The Christian says, however, that he
was a miraculous conception as to his humanity
and that he was really the only begotten and eternal Son of God. Here then upon inferential
facts they widely differ. · Let the candid and yet
undetermined then take the facts that are admitted on all hands, and reason whether he will be
an unbelieving Jew or believing Christian. Let

him ask himself thus: What inducement had the judicious Joseph to retain his espoused Mary and take such care of her son, if the fact be not as the christian scriptures declare? It is well known that jealousy is the rage of a man, and that it will frequently sunder the bands of matrimonial connection, when these have been strengthened by long intimacy, and mutual pledges of everlasting attachment. Here every facility of alienation was afforded. The law was in his favour if the fact of the espousal had been as it commonly was public.* In this instance, however, it seems he had it in his power and in his mind to put her away privately. Why did he not? the Christian has a reason—an angel appeared to him and told that although his espoused Mary was pregnant, yet she was also a virgin, and that she was with child of the Messiah according to the scriptures, a virgin shall conceive; a woman shall compass a man. The Jew has none. Although descended of the royal family of David she was no heiress. That family was reduced, she had neither money nor friends even in her own city, when she was enrolled according to the decree of Cæsar Augustus, but must endure, even in her delicate situation, the hardships of a stable lodging. Her offering was the offering of the poor. Soon was the babe, her mother, and reputed father exposed also to persecution. When Herod understood

* That espousal was a public deed generally, and so an example for the orderly practice observed in civilized communities generally of publishing parties before marriage, is evident from this fact, that the punishment of violating the betrothed was the same as for adultery. Deut. xxii. 24.

from the wise men, that some great personage was born at Bethlehem, where the Priests and Levites told the Messiah should be born.   He sought the young child's life, and Joseph must travel with his espoused wife into Egypt.   How will the Jew account for this?   That Joseph should be so careful of one that was, as they blaspheme, a bastard, illegitimate!!   But further, his friends and himself hold out uniformly this idea that he was the Son of God.   The Jews do not assert that he enjoyed any distinguishing opportunities of learning, how is it then that he was so successful in procuring not only the temporary approbation of the doctors, and the applause of the people, but also the destruction of their system, and the dispersion of the Jews.   If not eminently favoured of God, was the thing possible for him ?   If not anointed with the Holy Ghost above measure?   Would God then countenance to such a degree, such an arch imposter, and audacious blasphemer as they make him to be?   Impossible :   They charge him with calling himself the Son of God, they reckon this the same as making himself God, or equal with God.   He neither denies the fact nor the inference of the charge. Again, they both say he was crucified between two thieves—both say he was laid in Joseph's tomb—both say the tomb stone was sealed and a watch or guard of Roman soldiers set, to prevent the disciples from stealing away the body by night.   They both agree that the body was removed, and that a great many believed he rose again. These are primary facts then upon which the disputants and opponents in this great controversy agree, facts which Jews and Greeks, Mahometans and Christians all admit as being established with more particular and ample evidence than can generally be obtained, or is generally asked for, in ascertaining facts of history. Then what are the inferential conclusions? Why the Jew says the disciples came by night when the guard slept and stole him away. The Christian says, he rose by the power of God. Here they widely differ, but it is upon a point in which you are not bound to give implicit credit to the testimony of either. You have an opportunity to decide from the internal evidence of the one or the other of the statements, from other occurrences of those times recorded without any counter testimony, from the effects which the embracing or rejecting of the one or other side has had. First then it is to be noticed that the christian scriptures have recorded without valid contradiction from Jewish and Gentile persecutors, the only rational way, by which this historical phenomenon can be accounted for, or explained. They say that the soldiers are hired to relate an inconsistent falsehood, viz. That while they slept the disciples stole away the body of Jesus. Now in the first place, it must be admitted that this was the account that was given of the matter by the soldiers, by the Jews, by the unbelieving world generally. It would necessarily produce a great deal of investigation. Some cause must be assigned why the body of Jesus was not in the tomb of Joseph. Again it was impossible that the disciples could preserve a record of the solution of this problem which was false. If the soldiers had not said that this was the case, it would have been easy for the Jews to have confuted at once this part of New Testament record. It was about a third party, viz. the Romans that were many ways more attached to, and interested in the Jewish credit now, rather than in the Christian. It must then be a matter of fact that the soldiers said this. The thing, then, to be examined is, did they say the truth? In solving this question we must take several things into the account. 1. What object could they have in view, if they could not save their living master how could the corps of their dead master do any thing for them? 2. Is it likely that the cowardly disciples who trembled and fled and basely denied their Master when interrogated by damsels, would dare, at night, to enter the defiles of a Roman guard, break the seal of the nation and remove the heavy stone, and bear away the dead body? 3. How could this bearing away a dead body avail to the shewing of the same body alive before many witnesses? But again, what does the saying of the guard testify? It says that they were guilty of death. Why were not the laws of the military code executed? It was death for one to sleep, and yet how did they all sleep? If they all slept, how did they know what was done? How came they then to tell this incoherent self contradictory story? The scriptures tell us they we're promised impunity, in the implied fault, and bribed to re-late the obvious falsehood.

If the great fact of our Saviour's resurrection then must be admitted, as the only resolution of the historical problems of that time, indifference to the publication of this truth cannot be either humane or religious. We should imitate the conduct of the disciples and saints, who witnessed to this truth, by administering and receiving all divine ordinances. What other principle can account for the determined stand they took in op-position to the world, at the peril of every thing which other men count dear? There was no possibility of their being mistaken or deceived in the numerous interviews they had with their ris-en Master. There is no possible motive which can be conceived, that could induce them to at-tempt the deception of others; and there is no possible way, by which their answer can be ac-counted for, in scattering the tribes of their Jew-ish and demolishing the empire and fanes of their Gentile enemies, but that their testimony was true and their cause the cause of God. It can-not be said they were designing knaves, for such characters have some object in view: what then was theirs? They had seen their master sus-pended upon the cross, they expected such an end themselves, and were not disappointed. Hav-ing no ground then to believe in a blessed resur-rection, to act in this manner was evidently super-lative madness and consummate folly. This be-

ing the case then, what are we to say of the two
classes of men, with whom they had to deal?
Many believed in them. They must, of course, be
counted at least as foolish as their foolish deceivers.
But what of those who opposed them? They
could not prevail by argument—they erect gibbets
for them and kindle furnaces to burn the maniacs.
Is this then the view that the advocates of man's
perfectibility and the humanity of heathens give
of these matters!!! Man is silly enough and
bad enough even when you tell the truth of him,
and exhibit his character in the light of candour
and charity.

But what do infidels who profess to vindicate
the justice of God say for that attribute, when the
fact is, that some how or other he made that religion prevail against all opposition? One of
themselves has long ago committed the fraterni-
ty. If it be of man it will come to naught; but
if it be of God ye cannot overthrow it. It has not
only not been overthrown, but it has overthrown
and will overthrow every thing else. And this it
has done, and will do, not by carnal weapons and
carnal policy. No, it has to guard itself against
all these: these ever have been, and ever will be
against it. By what, then, has it been so mighty,
if not through God? And can we safely set ourselves against that which he conserves, which he
sanctions by his providence, and seals by his
grace?

. But you will say, we object not to the truth of
religion. We only desist from a participation

and observance of its rites because of the party
spirit which prevails among professors. Religion, we admit, is something internal, and unless it
influence life and morals it cannot be genuine ;
and yet we contend that it is presumptive and
dangerous to neglect the positive institutions of
piety. It is contrary to our nature to observe no
rituals;—it is extremely ungrateful to neglect
God's appointments ;—it is by no means safe to
violate positive institutions. The nation has never been found, in which there is no religious ceremonies observed. It is quite a reasonable service to offer our souls and bodies a living sacrifice holy and acceptable upon the altar of divine
institution. Has God graciously appointed these
appropriate ordinances, and yet shall we neglect
them ? Has our Creator, Preserver and Saviour
no claims on our gratitude ? Obedience is of
this principle the best evidence, " If ye love me
keep my commandments." What was it that
first " brought death into the world and all our
woe." Was it not man's first disobedience in
violating a divine institution ? Would that soldier be considered a dutiful soldier who would
refuse to wear the livery of his country ? If
Christ commanded such rites generally to be observed, what valid reason can we give for omis-
sion ? If they who sinned against Moses' law
died, at the mouth of two or three witnesses, of
how much greater punishment shall he be thought
worthy, who shall either profanely use, or sullenly
neglect these solemn rites by which the blood of

the covenant is signified, sealed and applied?
Are the men of this generation stiff necked and
rebellious? There is the more need that all who
are his friends, should show themselves friendly,
and not reject the counsel of God against themselves by refusing to be baptised in his name. If
any man shall be ashamed of him, of his truth or
of his ordinances in the midst of this crooked and
perverse generation, of him will he be ashamed
when he shall come in his own glory and in his
Father's. Do you ask, then, what you shall do
to be saved? We are commisioned to preach the
gospel of good tidings to every creature, giving
them this assurance, that he that believeth and is
baptized shall be saved. We have Apostolical example to say "Repent and be baptized every one of
you in the name of Jesus for the remission of sin,
and ye shall receive the gift of the Holy Ghost;
for the promise is to you and to your children
and to all that are afar off, even as many as the
Lord our God shall call." Should you say, if
you have the spirit of true religion, you need not
be much concerned about rites and forms, you
will not thereby shun the vortex of controversy.
There is a denomination who say so: the Quakers say there is but one baptism, and seeing there
is certainly an inward spiritual baptism there
can be need of any outward. But they might
just as well argue that man is but one; there is a
spirit in man, or an inward man; therefore there
is no necessity of mending the outward man or
body. They pretend to reject all instituted forms

Z

of religion; but even they have some forms. They
have their drab coloured and buttonless coats as
the badge of their religion. They reason contrary to the Apostles. They forbid water to their
disciples and say they have the spirit. The A-
postles say, " Can any man forbid water that
these should be baptized who have received the
Holy Ghost as well as we." Acts x. 47. You
see then that uniform custom and divine institution enjoin the observance of rites of religion.
But you will say, I have not the spirit, and therefore I cannot with propriety be baptized, and
make a profession of what I do not posses. If
you do not, you ought. Will it answer as an excuse to God, that you were not disposed to bear
faithful and true allegiance to your heavenly potentate? Has he not made his revelation credible? Why do you not believe it with your
heart? This is his command: It is a reasonable
command, and if you do, you may be baptized according to express commandment and indubita-
ble precedent. If you do not, you know the awful
consequence. Cry then, Lord I believe, help my
unbelief. With the heart man believeth unto
righteousness, and with the mouth confession
is made unto salvation. The Lord added
unto the church only such as should be saved.
The manner in which you should observe this
initiatory ordinance, you must learn from what
has been already said, and from what we are a-
bout briefly to lay down, for the direction of this
second division of the undetermined, viz. They

who have never been baptized, feel convictions of
the truth and impression of the importance of religion, and yet are undecided about scriptural
forms. We feel sensibly for your case. It is
painful to halt between two opinions. It is
natural for every person who is a subject of divine grace, to be inquisitive about divine truth
and instituted order, and of course to say solemnly, " Lord, what wouldst thou have me to do ?".
This enquiry will be minute in proportion as im-
aginations are brought into the obedience of faith.
Haughty unsubdued minds will always have
something to say in its religion. The true christian will act as Eli directed Samuel, saying, Lord
speak for thy servant heareth. At the same time
that this is a laudable disposition, it may be carried too far, or rather another may be mistaken for
it. There may be a zeal without knowledge.
Much litigation has been in the Churches about
opinions and rites of human invention. This is
not the error however of the present day. If
then it were the ease that God had commanded
you to be dipped, I trust my gracious Master
would not allow me to forbid you. If he had
commanded you to leave your children without
when you came in, I trust I should not invite
you to bring them. Let this matter then be seriously examined. Try both sides ; lay by prej-
udices. Try to imbibe as much of the spirit of
the gospel as possible, and let these subjects be
decided when you are most under its influence.
See whether the admission or rejection of the in-

fants of believers would be the greatest evidence of divine grace, condescension, and kindness to the children of men; or, whether the subjects, administrators and spectators of baptism may not be as composed and believing and of course as much edified by the affusion or sprinkling of water upon the body of the baptized as by plunging it under the water; whether this will not answer as well for a symbol of what it is designed to signify, allowing the scriptures to be the judges, in this case, of propriety. If there be many instances in scripture phrase wherein the operation of the spirit in applying the blood of Christ is expressed by sprinkling, and none where the same is expressed by dipping, you will be at no loss to decide which mode is most eligible, convenient, expressive and proper. That cunning disputants upon the other side may be able to involve you in some difficulties, may be expected. There is nothing, as far as I know, but what in the present, partial, and imperfect knowledge of man, but what by subtle cavil may be somewhat involved in difficulty. "Now we see through a glass darkly." We may be practically, savingly and comfortably persuaded of many truths, against which notwithstanding there might be objections offered that we could not readily answer. Philosophers, or rather cavillers, of past centuries, brought forward objections, some against the existence of the material, some against the spiritual, world; which objections and cavils, required the patience and deep investigation of a Reed to answer, and yet I suppose, no honest man of common sense 'was made really skeptical about the evidence of his senses in regard to the visible world ; or of his consciousness and reflection in regard to the spiritual. Speculative triflers' have always been ingenious in throwing stumbling blocks in the way of sound philosophy and right religion, while the experimental philosopher and practical Christian have held on their way. Thus if you be careful to walk in the ways of piety and virtue as far as you know, God will reveal in you from time to time whatever may be necessary for the credit of true religion, and the comfort of your own heart. Wrestle with Jacob and you will prevail with Israel, in obtaining a promise of God's being not only your own God, but also the God of your seed. Christ loves importunity and ingenious reasoning, whereby he may be, as it were, compelled to shew kindness even to our seed. See the instance of the Syrophenician woman. She was not of the Jews, and therefore Christ reasoned with her, as if it had been improper that any thing should be done for her child. It is not meet to take the children's bread and cast to the dogs. What does she answer ? Truth Lord, yet the dogs eat of the crumbs which fall from the Master's table: See how Christ approves of her ingenious importunity, for he hates putting away; "O woman great is thy faith." Math. xv. 28— Mark vii. 29. "Verily," says he, on another similar occasion, "I have not found so great faith, no not in Israel." In this way, dear fellow

z 2

men I would have you to become determined, im-
portunate and resolute, so that you would not only come yourselves, and take the kingdom by
force for yourselves, but also bring your children, exercise faith upon the promise which is
to you and to your children, if you observe the
divine call. Be not troubled if some who are
called disciples, strive to keep your offering back.
The God of Israel hates putting away, he is willing and ready yet to be the God of your seed.
His hand is not shortened; his mercy is not diminished; his grace is yet great. He yet gathers the lambs in his arms, and will not *you* put
in for *your babes* ? If you approve of the covenant, would you not wish your babes to have a
share in it, and would you not wish that the grace
of God and the sprinkling of the blood of Christ
for their redemption should, publicly, in the sacrament of baptism, be acknowledged. You have
been active, if parents, in presenting to the world
children of the first Adam, labour in faith and
prayer that they may be born again, made children of Christ the second Adam. If you are
believers you are encouraged to do this. " Concerning your sons and your daughters, command
ye me :" Doing your duty according to the vow
implied in this act of representation and depend-
ing upon the grace which, in Christ Jesus, is
adapted for every case, you have nothing to fear.
" Train up a child in the way he should go, and
when he is old he will not depart from it." You
may err in calculating too low, but you can hard-

ly err in calculating too high upon the grace and mercy of God toward your seed. Only, think what God is, and what he has revealed himself to be through Jesus Christ; all that he promises to be to you and your seed!! Can you excuse yourselves if you are still among the fearful, and unbelieving, who refuse his offers and reject his counsel? Can you justify your conduct to your God or to your children if you receive not such gracious offers in their behalf, if you neglect to have their ears bored and nailed to the door of such a master! To be made children of God is better than all earthly nobility: to be made members of his church is better than to be citizens of any commonwealth; to have an inheritance among them who are sanctified in Christ Jesus, is better than to be heirs of any worldly patrimony!!

We must, before we finish our address to the undetermined, and with it, our book, say something to the third class, which is composed of those who have been baptized in their youth, and yet by the arguments of Anabaptists are undetermined in their minds upon this important point of controversy.

I hope I shall never be so far an enemy to truth as to urge implicit faith to any instruction merely human or continuance in any system that is predicated on the mere dogmas of man. To discuss the doctrines, with which our memories were stored in early youth, is laudable. The constitution of our nature, and the developement of

our mental powers seem to be an index of what
is our proper course of conduct in this respect.
Youth is docile in perception, capacious in memory, and credulous in believing; more advanced
life should be marked for abstraction, reasoning,
and investigation. If this mode be not adopted,
truths which have a divine basis and are predicated upon the scriptures, may have *to us*, nothing
for their foundation but the traditions of our
fathers and the dogmas of our teachers. I would
h ve you, therefore, shun this degrading extreme;
if the system which your parents taught you be
t ue, consistent and scriptural, it can bear an examination; if not, it is worth very little or rather
as a religious system, it is worth nothing at all.
If society around had all been taught as you were,
and you and they were disposed to continue in
that sys em, in which you had been taught, it
might be enough for the maintenance of any argument that could occur in that case, that you
know the current and catholic doctrines; but
seeing the Head of the Church has seen proper
that matters should be otherwise, you are under a
strong obligation to yourself and your system, to
give this and every other common controversy a
careful investigation, so that you may be prepared to give an answer to him that asks of you a
reason of your hope. As an inducement to investigation, also, I assure you that you never can
have the same comfort in believing any system
which you have taken upon the credit of others,
as you can have in the faith and profession of

that which you have examined, and discovered to have a scriptural foundation. The Thessalonians were believers and saved : They gave themselves, in a solemn covenant, first to God, and afterwards to his ministers by the will of Christ.*
The Apostle had reason to thank God for them, " because God had from the beginning chosen them to salvation through sanctification of the Spirit and belief of the truth."† Yet they were deficient in this respect and inferior to the Bereans. Why ? Because these latter searched the scriptures daily, whether these things were so. At the same time, however, that we would encourage investigation, we would dissuade from either a precipitate change or constant indecision. The latter of these will be the native result of the former as well as of a partial investigation of the subject. Whilst all rapid and thoughtless charges are improper and dangerous, there are some things peculiarly critical in the change which your indecision, if not settled, contemplates. Let us view a few of them.

. 1st. It is an act of the greatest ingratitude and dishonour to your parents, who in your infancy had you solemnly dedicated to God by the symbol of the sprinkling of the blood of Christ. Are you then solicitous to nullify their deed and to declare that their offering was an abomination ? Are you prepared to say that parents have no right to make a religious disposal of their children ? If you despise the religious transac-

* 2 Cor. viii.   † 2 Thes ii. 13.

tions of your parents, and scorn to have church
privileges entailed to you through their representation, you ought, to be consistent, to renounce all
other advantages which have, or might have
accrued to you through the same channel. Now,
how would you do in another case? Suppose
through them were assigned to you as their heirs
a large estate; would you say that you would
have nothing but what you earned by labor or
gained by trade? I trow not. Then evidently,
if you renounce the inheritance, you will be considered as despising your birthright, as well as
your parents, and I would really have you take
care lest you seek its restoration in vain, should
you seek it again even by tears.

But in the second place. By acting in the way
which Anabaptists would have you, you excommunicate all Pedobaptist professors. Are you
prepared to say that none are baptized but those
whom Anabaptist elders dip? If so, you must
look upon surrounding professors not only as unbaptized heathens, but as arrogant profaners of
a very holy ordinance. I say you must consider
them as wilful opposers of the purity of divine
institutions, because I cannot conceive, how you
could find for them the apology of comparative
ignorance. Baptists themselves must admit that
the ministers of other denominations are at least
equal in learning to theirs. Now, do you really
think that all the fathers of the first ages of the
christian church, who contended so earnestly for
the faith once delivered to the saints, who vindi-

cated so bravely the prophetic office of Christ against the traditions of the Jews and the philosophy of the Gentiles, were either not taught of God themselves, or were such knaves that they would deceive others by baptizing those who neither were, nor could be the subjects of that ordinance? Their success in confuting all the learning and all the policy of that day, confutes the first of these suppositions ; the fact that in maintaining their system, in vindicating the liberty whereby Christ makes his people free, they had to resist unto blood, striving against sin, renders the latter of these suppositions, namely, their insincerity, impossible. It is true this controversy had then no place in the Church. Those who had been engrafted into the good olive tree, had no doubt but that if the root was holy so were the branches. They knew that in the Apostolic churches the children even of a pious mother were holy, not by native innocence, not by works of righteousness, but by the washing of regeneration and the renewing of the Holy Ghost, which was promised to be poured out upon the seed of believers. What are we to say of that galaxy of burning and shining lights that rose upon the benighted world at the reformation ? Can you mention any of those who have attained to eminence for that great work, that were advocates or rather that were not strenuous opposers of that system which excludes from the Church of the Redeemer the infant, seed of believers ? Were we now to write in this controversy in the style

in which Luther, Calvin, Owen and Flavel have
discussed this subject we would be thought very
harsh. These men, too, did not draw their arguments from the practice of the Church in the
middle and dark ages, but from the authority of
the primitive fathers, from the Apostles and
prophets, on which foundation they uniformly desired to build, Jesus Christ himself being the
chief corner stone. Were these men then ignorant and weak, or were they roguish and deceit-
ful men! They had all the weight of arguments
that have been since adduced in favour of that
system, they were in the way of reformation;
they had no long formed attachments to any system but to the one they renounced. In what way
then are we to account for their practice, but that
they were persuaded that truth permitted, yea,
encouraged the admission of infants into the
Church in the simple, plain, but at the same time,
expressive and scriptural mode of baptism by affusion. Before, then, you renounce either the
doctrines or order of these eminent reformers,
whose integrity was equal to their talents, and
their talents and integrity equalled by few, I have
but one thing to ask of you, viz. That you first
know their system, and that then you act prayer-
fully and conscientiously. Doing so, I have no
fear, that you will either excommunicate them, or
renounce the scriptural system which from them
has been to you, in kind Providence, transmitted.
Hold fast then what you have received; let no
man take your crown: for he established a testi-

mony in Jacob and appointed a law in Israel,
which he commanded our fathers that they should
make them known to their children ; that the generation to come might know them ; even the children which should be born ; who shall arise and
declare them to their children.   In the third
place if you should adopt the Anabaptist system,
you must be again baptized.   If that would be
necessary in your case, it would be necessary in
the case of all who have been baptized in infancy ;
if it would not be necessary in, all cases, and yours
being the same as theirs, it must be a profanation
of the name of God and of the ordinance of baptism.   You can easily see then, that whether you
will or not your infant baptism puts you in a predicament very different from that of those who
have not been subjects of that solemn rite.   You
will, perhaps, say, you cannot answer the Baptist
objections against infant baptism.   What then ?
Is there no way of accounting for this, but that
they are unanswerable ?   Can you answer all the
objections of the deist against the scriptures and
the Christian religion ?   If you cannot ; have you
not the same reason to become a deist that you
have to become an Anabaptist ?   Again—should
you change you change your profession to-mor-
row are you sure that you could answer all the
objections which might be brought against the
system ?   If so, you will, to be sure, be so far
comfortable ; if not, what better will you be then
than you are now ?   The same obligation will be
upon you to change that is now, but this difficulty

A a

will be in the way, that you do not want to be always changing, and you will have a kind of pride in maintaining a system which you have personally adopted. You may say, however, that you shall then be baptized in a way which you are sure is scriptural, and therefore your mind will be easy. It will certainly be desired by all true christians that they may profess what is true, and practise what is correct, according to the scriptures; but you will find it to be a very hard task to bring from scripture any precedent of the same deed that you have in contemplation. There were adults baptized; of that we have no doubt. So we, without any scruple, baptize adults, of whose cordiality in the faith of the gospel, we can obtain comfortable evidence: But where is the example of any baptized in adult years who had been baptized in infancy? This is your case, and for this you have no scriptural precedent. Nay more, until the fifteenth or sixteenth century, you will find no precedent of this kind, and at that time it need not seem strange, when society received such a fiery purgation, if some dross should be found among those who were separated from the popish mass. You will perhaps further object, that sprinkling a little water upon an unconscious babe could answer no purpose for the purging of the soul. It is admitted on all hands that baptism, in whatever form, and to whatever subjects administered, does not avail to the purifying of the flesh, or the cleansing of our polluted, carnal nature. It is only by the blessing of God upon an ordinance of his own that we can expect any advantage from the sacraments. Is God then not able to bless the infants of his people with effusions of his Spirit for cleansing and sanctification according to his own promise? If so, are we not bound to acknowledge this his great grace and condescension, and having had it acknowledged upon ourselves, we ought certainly not to deny it, either in its propriety, or to our offspring. Do you yet object that you have found no advantage from your baptism, and therefore you consider it necessary that you should renounce the first and have recourse to another baptism? Before you actually do so, I would ask you a few questions. First—Have you improved your infant baptism as you ought? If you have, and yet find no advantage I could not much blame you for trying an adult baptism. If you have not; then, Second—I would ask you, whether it is not likely that the calamity of your spiritual condition is to be ascribed to your misimprovement of a divine ordinance, than that infant baptism is destitute of authority? You know, there is no propriety in reasoning from the abuse of any thing against its right observation and use. In the old dispensation circumcision was profitable to those who kept the law of that institution; in relation to others, circumcision became uncircumcision; not so that the rite should be repeated, of which we have no record, but that they might not, in a licentious course, presume upon covenant blessings, but rather take warning and reform. The same is the case here. If we have trampled under-foot the blood of the covenant; there is no other blood of atonement; nor any propriety of having baptism, the symbol thereof, either in the same, or any other form, repeated. Third—Should you proceed to make the rash experiment, and run the hazardous, because unauthorized, risk, Are you sure that you will keep perfectly the vows and obtain certainly the advantages of religion in this second and other baptism? If you are, then go on and prosper: If not, Is one profanation and misimprovement not enough? Are you prepared to say, that God cannot consistently give you the comforts and blessings of salvation if you walk in all the statutes and ordinances of religion, according to the obligations of your first baptism, unless you have recourse, without any argument direct or indirect for this unauthorised deed? I would really have you take care, and look before you leap, lest you find yourself not only plunged in waters of affliction, but lest you should also be mired in a morass of delusion and carnal calculation, from which extrication will be difficult. Are you prepared to say, that your parents had no right to dedicate you to God by baptism; or that if they had, you have a right to disannul, as far as you can, their deed? Are you prepared to say, that all your pious predecessors were unbaptized heathens; either blind and ignorant, or rebellious and obstinate, and that all who satisfy themselves with in-

fant baptism do, either ignorantly or wilfully, reject the counsel of God against themselves by
refusing to receive a christian baptism? Have
you lived so long without noticing one mark and
evidence of providential or gracious kindness,
which might restrain you from renouncing the
covenant God of your youth? Has he ever
commanded you, or any of the seed of Jacob, to
seek his face in vain? Rather, Has he not a thousand and a thousand times saved you from dan-
gers, and granted you supplies, for which you neither prayed, nor gave him thanks? Can you
then be so foolish, and, ungrateful as even to try to
get another God than this God of your fathers,
and God of your youth? Would it indeed be
an advantage to barter the God of Abraham,
Isaac and Jacob for any of these modern deities,
that thoughtless man has made? Is it an attribute against which you would object, that He is
the God of his people's *seed?* If your present
indecision be likely to have that termination, it
would, certainly, be proper that you should give
him some other name, as well as ascribe to him
other attributes. The God of Israel is the maker
of all things. If you choose *another,* whatever
you may call him, he must be inferior, yea, if we
allow the scriptures to be judge, in the case, they
will tell us that the gods who did not make the
heavens are no Gods. Nor must you call him
Christ, for he is the same who appeared to Abraham and to Moses. Before Abraham was, says he,
I AM. Against whom did Israel rebel; whom

did they tempt.? Certainly it was Jehovah their God. yet the Apostle, has most positively said that they tempted Christ. 1. Cor, x. 9. " Neither let us tempt Christ as some of them also tempt-ed." This need not seem strange, for he is the same in all ages past, present, and to come. Heb. xiii. 8. " Jesus Christ the same yesterday, to day and for ever." If you adopt another than the God of Israel as your God, either the God of Is-rael is not the true. God, or yours is not; for there is, and can be, but one true God. *Hear, O Israel, the Lord our God is one Lord. There is one God, and one Mediator, between God and man, the Man Christ Jesus.* If you join another Church, than that which was in the wilderness you cannot join the true Church, unless there be more true churches than one ; Christ Jesus the divine Hus-band has but one spouse—one Church, and in that Church he will have his children named, and nourished, recognized and cherished. Can you then any longer hesitate and be undetermined— will you not from this time say; " Thou art my Father the guide of my youth ?" Would you not sustain a loss to relinquish all the precious prom-ises, and lose the sanction of all the salutary pre-cepts of Old Testament scriptures ? And how can you retain the new, which so fully and fre-quently establishes the authority of the old? Can the cause be good or eligible, which requires such a sacrilege and such a sacrifice? Try the reasoning of those, who are like to persuade you, and see if they do not lead to such conclusions.

I do not say, they either profess, or intend it.
Neither is it certain that they will admit the inferences, which from their system may fairly be
deduced.   That being the case, I would not even
charge them with holding these tenets.   Still, I
insist that the system leads to them; and numbers,
by reflecting and arguing upon the system have
actually professed them.   If I know any thing of
my own heart too, I can assure you it is with
pain that I have even glanced at the consequences
of a system which so many, bearing the christian
name defend and maintain.   There are many of
the profession, against which I have been writing,
of whom I would charitably hope the better things
that accompany salvation, though I thus speak.
The scriptures leave it without a doubt, that all
who build upon a right foundation shall be saved,
although they may heap upon that foundation of
Christ Jesus; a great deal of stubble, which they
must, in the end, be willing to have consumed.
It is because I love their persons, and, in many
respects their deportment, that I feel such an interest in having their dreams and delusions destroyed.   " What is the chaff to the wheat?"   If,
too, we were to hesitate about joining a system as
long as we see any of its vouchers apparently
pious, we might hesitate long, and about many systems.   When we make a profession it should not
be of our own piety, or of the piety of our party ;
but it should be of our faith in Jesus Christ the
only Saviour, the living and true God.   If you
would attain a comfortable establishment of heart

in a profession of religion you must examine carefully your own heart to make your calling and election sure, but; I do not know that you have any authority to examine the heart and experiences of others. It is by their intelligent profession, and holy walk and conversation, that is, *by their fruits ye shall know them.* There are, alas! too many instances of proof to shew that men may call themselves converted christians, when yet they make the true Christ a blasphemer as did the Pharisees of old, because he, being a man makes himself *equal* to God. Proselyting zeal and ostentatious piety may run very high where there is no true religion. *And when he was demanded of the Pharisees when the kingdom of God should come, he answered them and said, the kingdom of God cometh not by observation; Neither shall they say; Lo here, or Lo there, for, behold the kingdom of God is within you. When they shall say to you, See here; or See there, go not after them nor follow them.* If there ever was a time in which it was necessary that the Spirits should be tried certainly it is now. Still if we humbly and diligently apply ourselves to this work, taking the bible as our manual, and the Spirit of God speaking therein as our guide, to the knowledge of all truth, we need not be like children tossed to and fro with every wind of doctrine; but may become strong in the faith, giving glory to God. Difficult as these trying times are, and scarce as true faith may be, undetermined and wavering people of God's covenant,

trust in the Lord and you shall yet be established." "Why sayest thou, O Jacob, and speakest
O Israel. My way is hid from the Lord and my
judgment is passed over from my God. Hast
thou not known, hast thou not heard that the everlasting God, the Lord, the Creator of the ends of
the earth fainteth not, neither is weary? there is
no searching of his understanding: He giveth power to the faint; and to them that have no might he
increaseth strength. Thus saith the Lord that
formed thee from the womb which will help thee;
Fearnot, O Jacob my servant; and thou Jesurun
whom I have chosen. For I will pour water upon him that is thirsty, and floods upon the dry
ground: I will pour my spirit upon thy *seed* and
my blessing upon thy *offspring;* And they shall
spring up as among the grass, as willows by the
water courses. Hearken unto me, O house of
Jacob, and all the remnant of the house of Israel,
which are borne by me from the belly, which are
carried from the womb; And even to your old
age I am he; and even to hoar hairs will I carry
you?" What say you, then, dear descendants
of God's people, do you still hesitate, whether or
not, you should be stedfast in God's covenant; or,
do you not rather say with David. "The Lord
hath made with me an everlasting covenant, ordered in all things, and sure, for this is all my salvation and all my desire."

FINIS.

INDEX.

INDEX.

ERRATA.

☞ In consequence of the haste in which the foregoing work was prepared for publication, and the distance of the Author's residence from the press, the following errors passed unnoticed:

Page 1. line 21, for *John* read *Matthew*

p. 3 l 9, for *decreed*, read *decried* —l 9 read *revolutionary*

p. 4 l.31 — read *Redeemer & Ruler,*

p 5, l 17, for *of* read *or.*

p. 15. l 1, — *Barrabas,* read *Barnabas.*

p 16, l. 20 for *Jew* read *Jewess.*

p. 19. l 25 for *ther's* read *these*

p. 20, l. 18, — *fathers by the prophets.*

p 21, l 27, — *in the first book*

p. 30, l 31, — *the great mass of mankind,*

p. 31, l 32, for *portion,* read *paction.*

p. 39, l 22, for *discern,* read *describe.*

p. 40, l 15, for *anoption,* read *adoption.*

p. 43, l. 16, for *Bibler* read *Bible* ; for *Hur* read *Alexander.*

p 47, l. 32, — read *have been granted.*

p 69, l. 15. — *whither* read *thither.*

p. 73, l. 17 — *ceremonial* read *formal.*

p. 80, l. 23. for *violation* read *violaters*

p. 84, l. 16, — *He was there* — *It was then* —same page, l 31, — *Son* — *Sun.*

p. 85, l. 1, read *This is the day in which, &c.*

p. 95 l 27, — *or* — *as.*

p. 100, l. 3, for *to* read *as.*

p. 100, l. 18 — *last* read *law.*

p, 109, l. 1. — *apothegym* read *apothegm.*

p. 133, l. 7, — *more cruel than was ever*

p 135, l 13 — *teach* — *touch*

p 135, l. 15 — *or considerably, so.*

p. 141, l. 25 — *passion* — *as' censton.*

p. 146, l. 8, — *that put a comma*

p 180, l 11, for *sarce* — *sacer.*

p. 183, l. 32, — *3d* — *53d.*

p. 190, i 31. read *Psalm li.* for *Isa. lii.*

p. 197. l 19 — *without* — *with.*

p. 220, l. 31, read *again, the advocate &c.*

p 228 l. 17 for *as* read *or.*

p. 237 l 2. Put the period after *solicitude,* and read, *At the bar of a practical public it may,*

p. 240, l 17 for *feuds* — *beads.*

p 241, l. 9 for *word* — *creed*

p. 243, l. 30 for *motion* read *motive.*

p. 245, l 25 for *blessing* read *blessings*

p. 252, l. 12, — *congregation* — *congregations.*

p. 258, l. 5, — *shew* — *stand.*

p. 259. l 1 — *iv.* — *vii.*

p. 259. l. 17. for *support* read *respect.*

p. 264, l. 24, — *lxxix* — *lxxxix.*

p. 265, l 3, — *Son* read *God.*

p 267, l 33 *cxiv.* — *cxliv.*

p. 268, l. 17, — *argument* — *agreement.*

p. 274, l. 20, — *answer* read *success.*

p. 275, l. 20, for *naught* read *nought.*

p. 276, l. 11, — *is* — *are.*

p. 277, l. 31, — *mending* read *minding:*

p. 278, l. 12, for *posses* read *possess.*

p. 279, l. 22 — *ease* — *case.*

p. 281, l. 19 for *charges* read *changes.*

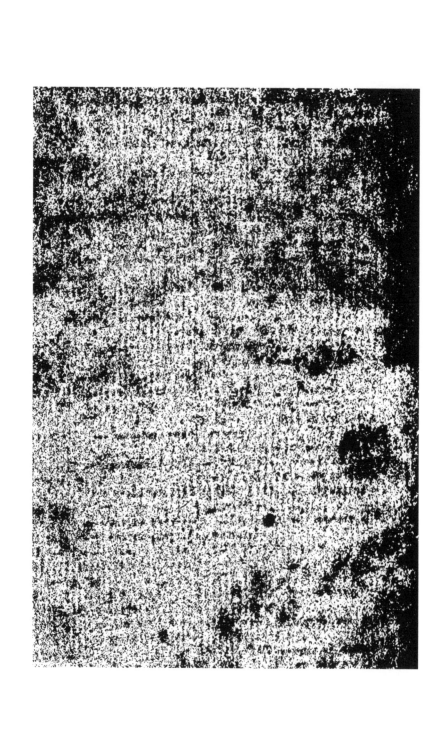

Lightning Source UK Ltd.
Milton Keynes UK
UKHW012221110219
337137UK00006B/1336/P